Stop Buying Bins

STOP BUYING BINS

& Other Blunt but Practical Advice From a Home Organizer

Bonnie Borromeo Tomlinson

Yellow Lab Press
AMHERST, MASS

Printed in the United States of America.

Editor: Kendra Adkins
Proofreader: Genevra Hanke
Book and cover design: David W. Edelstein
Author photograph: Yellow Lab Press
Cover illustration uses a resource from Freepik.com

Yellow Lab Press
Amherst, MA 01002

Library of Congress Control Number: 2021921933

ISBN: 978-1-7378818-0-3 (paperback)
ISBN: 978-1-7378818-1-0 (ebook)

Subjects:
Nonfiction | How-To | House and Home |
Self-Help | Organizing | Downsizing
HOM019000

For Gilly

And for my high school critical writing teacher
who sadly passed during the writing of this book,
the late Mr. Ronald Cecere,
whom I have often credited in conversation with
inspiring me to write.

Acknowledgments

When I open a book for the first time, I like to start with the acknowledgments. More times than not, there is a list of names—agents, editors, publishers—being thanked for their part in the business of the book. But every once in a while, there is a glimpse into the author's life that makes me smile in the knowledge that what I'm reading is the sharing of a personal journey. That's what this was for me. And these are the people I have to thank for their support along the way.

Thank you to Kendra Adkins, owner of Four Seasons Books in Shepherdstown, West Virginia, and yes, regardless of what I said just moments ago, my editor. Our relationship started out professionally, but our first meeting felt more like old friends catching up over coffee. I felt an instant bond with you and I know the universe put you on my path to show me what direction to take. You encouraged me to sign up for my first writer's conference, which opened my eyes to the fact that I could indeed do this. You read my first pages and said, "I'm hungry for more," which lit the fire in me to make this book a priority. I can't thank you enough. Thank you.

Thank you to Deborah Zavos, my former therapist, who in the autumn of 2019 said, "What would you like your life to look like a year from now?" And without hesitation I replied, "I would like to be a writer living in Amherst, Massachusetts." I will be forever grateful to you for making me proudly articulate out loud what I never had the courage to mutter internally before. Thank you.

Thank you to Ryan Pinkston, my former colleague, my sarcastic soul sibling, my sounding board, and one of my very besties, who regularly serves me the tough love I need—heavy on the love. You've talked me out of mistakes so many times I've lost count. Thank you, my friend.

And thank you to too many friends to name individually (well, maybe just a few: Julie Marshall, Denise Strafaci, Randy Elkinson) who continually checked in on my progress, which was immensely helpful because more times than not I was procrastinating. Thank you also to the "friends" who made it clear they didn't think this project was anything more than a waste of time—being underestimated has always been my biggest motivator.

And lastly, thank you to my daughter (and a far better writer than I), Gillian Blair Tomlinson. This is more of an apology than a thank you. Thank you for putting up with me. I know what a royal pain I can be when life is hectic and out of sorts. And since it's just the two of us, you take the brunt of it all (occasionally I yell at the dog, but you know she's not listening). I hope that any issues I've passed down to you are easily explained away by a professional mental health expert and that it makes your own writing better. I am exceedingly proud of the person you are and what part I had in getting you here. You are the person I want to be when I grow up. I love you.

If you are not listed in my acknowledgments, that does not mean, by any stretch of the imagination, that I am not grateful for you in my life. Everyone in my life, even on the periphery, affects who I am and how I write. You are part of the whole. And I am truly grateful.

Why You Should Read This Book: A Note from the Author

As I sit to write this note from the author, I am barricaded in my bedroom with my dog, Athena, while there are painters in several rooms on several levels of my house. I'm two months away from putting my house on the market. A house, that by the time I move, I will have lived in for 20 years—the longest period of time I've ever lived in one place. This house has seen a typical family life: two very sheddy white dogs, violent morning sickness, a four-month kitchen remodel that nearly killed me, a divorce so respectful that it did not, and more than a few paint colors, which after this week will all be neutral.

Last month I left my day job. I thought it best to be unencumbered by a work schedule (and by unfortunate association, a paycheck) to focus on some life-changing personal turning points:

- downsizing, renovating, and selling my house before moving out of state;
- preparing my only child for her last year of high school and onto college; and

- following through on my secret lifelong dream of being a writer.

Apparently tackling all of life's milestones at the same time is how I do things.

Writing this book about downsizing while I myself am downsizing is purely coincidental, but I couldn't have asked for better timing! While I've helped many clients with large-scale minimizing projects, I've never had the need to do my own hard-target purge until now. And since looming in the not-so-distant future is a house half the size of the one I'm currently in, I've been paring down in anticipation of significantly less elbow room. Some items have gone to friends, others were sold at a charity estate sale; most, however, were dropped at my local thrift store, where up to three times a week the guys at the donation center started clearing space in the warehouse upon seeing my car. I've gotten rid of a lot!

But what does all this mean for this diminutive book? (I'm trying not to add to your clutter, after all.) It means that upon hearing the advice I have doled out over the years come back to me in my own voice, I'm happy to report that I passed; the advice I've given is sound. Thank goodness! (Especially since this book was conceived with the simple goal of helping people overcome their clutter—and if I couldn't use my own guidelines in an efficient manner, how could I expect anyone else to?)

So now, armed with the skills I've acquired through

trial and error, working with (and more importantly, listening to) clients, AND having put those skills to a personal test in my own home, I've recognized a distinct pattern. The pushback I've received from clients with regard to their stuff comes down to three obstacles over and over again:

- Decluttering our homes can be difficult.
- Letting go of things can be challenging.
- Living with less seems impossible.

My hope all along has been to break down these obstacles into easy, manageable steps—steps that tackle our resistance to downsizing the possessions in our lives before even considering plunging headlong into the act of physically purging. That personal internal work comes first because above all else, letting go of our things IS personal, not practical. The difficulty lies not in the actual value of these items but in the value we assign to them. Sometimes we convince ourselves of the emotional need to hold onto something for truly silly (even stupid) reasons. This book is ultimately an exercise in assigning appropriate real value to our objects and releasing ourselves from the burden of "more." I'm not here to judge, but I will put a mirror up to your reality so you can see your own situation for what it is—an obstacle to a better-functioning lifestyle.

We've all fallen victim to one or more of the following patterns, myself included. And to prove that point, Chapter 1 is all mine! Just enjoy the tales of "too much" in the chapters ahead, say to yourself "Oh, that's so me," and read on. The roots of this book are filled with practical advice and solutions based on actual situations that arise repeatedly in the home organizing world. This process may not be easy, either emotionally, psychologically, or physically, but when you are through, you won't know how you could have lived any other way.

Contents

Introduction

The tales I could tell about the houses I have been in would make your skin crawl. There was the walk-in closet with the scattered "adult" toys. And the bachelor pad with the kitchen cabinets of sneakers. And I will never forget (no matter how hard I try) the hoarder house where I slid across the grease-covered kitchen floor... I threw those shoes away.

But I'm not here to tell you horror stories. I'm here to tell you that no matter your end goal, be it living like a minimalist or just being able to find your kids' discarded socks before laundry day, living with less overall is the absolute first step to getting organized. Even with the most basic sense of spatial relations, if you have more stuff than space, it's not going to fit.

I can sense that you are already getting aggravated. How dare I suggest you have too much? Or that you need to let stuff go? Or that you should stop adding to the heap? Go ahead, hit me with a comeback. I've heard it all. In fact, I'd say there is a list of common responses that all clients have given at one point or another as an almost canned reaction as to why their homes are in the state they are in. Whether their houses run from just a few things out of place to full-on biohazard, one or more have been uttered in defense of the mess. And I've got the blunt but honest replies locked and loaded and listed in the following chapters. I by no means wish to belittle anyone who has or will proclaim one of these misguided excuses. I only want to highlight this one all-important point:

Your home is in disarray.
How you got there is the reason for the mess,
but not the reason for staying in it.

And with that said, let's take these one at a time. It is my hope that by the end of this book, you will not only have learned some practical ways to purge your possessions down to a manageable amount, but you will appreciate those things you do keep all the more.

FACT: You CANNOT organize your home if
you have more stuff than space.
The ABSOLUTE first step to organizing
is downsizing.

So yes, those acid washed jeans from 1986? Those have to go!

1

If It Doesn't Fit, Get Rid of It

Client: "This side of the closet is all my skinny clothes. I'm going to get back into them one of these days."

BBT: (smiles)

Maybe they remind you of happy memories, or they cost a small fortune, or they come with some hilarious buying story (my sisters and I have a ton of those). Whatever your reason, the list of excuses for holding onto clothes you no longer wear, or in some cases never wore at all, is exhaustive. I myself held onto the sweater I wore on my first date with my ex-husband, through our 20-year marriage, before telling myself, "I am NEVER going to wear this mock turtleneck again. I mean, dear Lord! Even if I could get back into a size 2, I wouldn't waste it on a mock turtleneck!"

* * *

Taking into consideration all the chaotic closet situations that I've worked on, I can say hands down that the number-one reason most clients hold onto clothes that they no longer wear is the agonizingly inaccurate "incentive" mentality—the holding onto of clothes, one-to-several sizes too small, as inspiration to get thin. It's a popular tool, and one that rarely if ever actually works. Of all the motivational measures you may find to lose weight, this isn't it. Believe me. I know all too well whereof I speak.

I'm in my 50s. As far as clothing sizes go I've worn them all from that aforementioned size 2 to an oversized 2XL. So I feel your pain when you say you want to hold onto your skinny clothes until "they fit again." In the meantime, they are actually working against you in more ways than one. And as painful as it may be to part with them, consider the self-torture you are inflicting on yourself every time you open your dresser drawers:

- These clothes are taking up room, room that could be devoted to clothes you can actually wear.
- These clothes are not acting as motivation, as one might think. Instead, they are a constant reminder of who you once were instead of who you are.

- They are a literal receipt of wasted money, which is just another way to fat-shame yourself.
- Fashion changes. Even classic clothes have a more current style. Getting back into something may not be worth it. (I told you about the mock turtle, didn't I?)
- As we age, our bodies change. Wearing that size again is one thing. Having it look good is another.
- If or when you do lose some weight, you will likely want to purchase new clothes to go with your new figure.
- Lastly and most importantly, nothing feels more defeating than opening the door to a closet overfilled with clothes and having nothing to wear.

For better or for worse, I had to work on this one myself. When my ex-husband and I first separated, I was looking to go back to work. I had been a stay-at-home mom for 10 years and my wardrobe consisted primarily of black yoga pants and oversized T-shirts. I was going to need to up my game if I wanted to secure a position with a DC-area decorator.

I had a few "career" pieces from my advertising days, but those were decades old and I didn't have a chance in hell of fitting into them anyway. "Why were you holding on to them in the first place?" you may ask wryly. For the same reasons you do: they were expensive, I wanted to be able to fit into them again, they were still in good condition, they reminded me of younger days, *blah blah whatever!* The fact is, though—they didn't fit, so they didn't deserve to take up space in my closet or, for that matter, my life.

In an act of unwavering determination—and to end the constant dismay of having a crowded closet but never anything to wear—**I pulled it all out!** Everything! From every closet and drawer and shelf. From all over the house. Shoes and coats and pajamas and bridesmaid gowns. If I was going to do this I was going to do it right, and that meant all or nothing. There was no halfway in that moment for me. I was all in! I even threw in a **load of laundry** just so I wasn't missing anything. Now in front of me was every piece of clothing I owned with the exception of what I was wearing. And even that I wasn't so sure I would be keeping.

Eagerly facing the mound amassed high on my bed, I started going through it item by item, **dividing everything into two simple piles—what fit and what did not**. Not what I wanted or needed or couldn't bear to part with. Not money spent, or memories attached, or the "but it's still good" refrain. NO, the only question was, **could I put it on my body?** And I didn't tell myself, "Oh, that fits," when I knew in my heart that getting it on and having it fit were two different things. This was an exercise in honesty with myself. There was no room for lying or pretending. This was going to be difficult and I was prepared for battle.

It started out pretty much as expected. Every piece that did not fit filled me with regret. The cocktail dress I wore to my cousin's wedding that I never had another reason to wear and now no longer could. That cropped sweater from college that I used to look so cute in that nowadays only accentuated my mommy midsection. The pants I got on sale that were never quite right to begin with but bought because I couldn't pass up that price. And with every piece I saw in my mind the money I'd spent. Some had tags, years old in fact, so I didn't even have to imagine. It was staring me right in the face. All the wasted money. All the wasted closet space. All the beating myself up for being too heavy to fit into the items of clothing that cost me money and took up space. All the regret for getting old and not living a life that kept me thin and gave me reason to wear those clothes that I wasted money on and that took up closet space. It's a deep, dark hole once you start digging down into the trench of regret. It seems easier to close the closet door and just keep wearing the clothes straight out of the laundry basket over and over. I know some of you reading this are really feeling me right now, and that it hurts. Deep breath, my friend. I understand and I'm here for you.

Regardless of the pain I was experiencing as the pile of "doesn't fit, won't fit, will never fit" was growing and toppling over onto the floor, I kept my goal in mind. Believe me, it wasn't all in strength, there were tears and a caffeine-fueled pity party or two. But nothing good comes from standing still. When it's hard, that's when you put your head down and keep going. Forging ahead, **I lumped together everything that did not fit and put it in another room.** Out of sight, out of mind. My ego was bruised, but I felt accomplished. And I rewarded myself with a quick 20-minute shuteye to regain my will to go on. Naps are the best!

Now back to what was in front of me. It was never more glaringly obvious that I was holding onto things that didn't serve me in any way than to see this sad, tiny assortment of make-do coordinates. Nearly 90% of what had been in my closet was now in another room, and it was time to get real with myself and **weed through the pile** in front of me. A pile of clothes that were too big and shapeless, or hung funny off my curvier parts, or were faded, pilling, or just plain ugly. There were so many mornings when I'd walk into my closet and just put on anything regardless of its attractiveness or how it made me feel to wear it. They were clothes just to cover my body. And now, faced with what I had truly been wearing for years, I had to admit I hated most of it. So I did what I had to do. **I added them to the "out" pile** in the other room.

What was left, I rehung. For a full week after, I didn't touch the pile in the other room. I didn't even look at it. Instead, every morning that week, I walked into what was now my essentially vacant closet and no matter what I put on, it fit, looked good, and made me just the slightest bit confident. No longer was I burdened by those "one day" or "can't part with them" clothes. I didn't have to try on endless items to find something comfortable, nor did I have to rehang everything that I tried on but didn't work. I didn't have to turn away from all the regret-provoking clothes to home in on the few useful pieces I had. And even though there was very little left, I was immediately surprised to find myself enjoying getting dressed each day. No more feelings of failure. I breathed easier, I held my posture better, I smiled more. Why? I hadn't lost weight or bought anything new. All I did was free myself from the self-inflicted punishment of stuff in my closet that no longer served any positive purpose. So what's next, you ask? What did I do with the clothes in the other room? Well, that part is easy.

Gift.
Donate.
Sell.

After that week had gone by and I hadn't missed any of it, I knew it all had to go. **Some went to friends** (the cocktail dress), **the bulk went to charity** (the cropped sweater), **a few pieces I held back to sell** (the pants that still had tags). But all of it was gone a few days later. And it was freeing! Did I have any regrets? Yes and no. I regretted making the mistake of keeping those things in the first place more than I ever did in giving them away. I didn't miss them at all. Why would I? I wasn't wearing them. Some I hadn't worn in decades. What then was I really missing? And that empty closet? It was looking like something staged for an organizing segment on morning TV where each piece hangs freely on its own barely touching the one next to it, all in color spectrum harmony.

* * *

Let me bottomline this for those of you just waiting for me to get to the bullet points. Don't start this project unless you can **devote the time to getting it done in one go around**, otherwise all you will have accomplished is pulling your mess out into the light of day and eventually having to sleep on it.

1. **Do the laundry.** You're going to want all your clothes in front of you for this project. That includes the week's worth of dirty socks in the hamper that in all honesty should just be thrown out because of the holes in the heels.

2. **Pull everything out of the closets and drawers from all over the house.** This includes everything from the ski jacket with the 30-year-old lift ticket on the zipper stored in the attic to the slippers from under your bed that are fuzzy with dust bunnies. Pants and activewear and

even undergarments get pulled out. You should be looking at everything.

ADVICE: Speaking of underthings, an ill-fitting bra changes everything from how your clothes hang on you to your overall posture. Several years ago, I started going to a bra shop where I was fitted by a professional. I found that the bras were not any more expensive than the ones I had previously bought in department stores and in the long run, far cheaper than the cheap bras that never fit right. It's well worth it and can ultimately be life changing. Nothing else matters but proper fit. Get rid of anything that doesn't.

3. **Separate your clothes into two piles.** There is only one question to ask yourself: "Does it fit?" Not "Could it fit?" or "Will it fit?" "<u>Does it fit?" Full stop!</u> I know you're saying, "But those are still good!" Well, yes, they are. But not for you. Don't bog yourself down with the value—monetary or emotional. For now, you just want a pile of clothes that you can wear and a pile that you can't.

4. **Take the out pile and put it in another room.** This is an experiment—out of sight, out of mind. They are not part of what you are doing now. Don't waste a moment thinking

about them or what you might eventually do with them.

5. **Break down the "does fit" pile.** There are a few more questions to ask yourself. Does it fit well? Is it attractive on? Is it in good condition? Do you still like it? Do you have any use for it? Answer NO to any of these questions and it gets added to the out pile. Keep only the items where the answer is YES to all questions.

6. **Everything that is a YES gets put neatly back in your closet and drawers.** Live out of your new collection of clothes for a week. **Wear them in rotation.** If there is anything that you consistently pass over, chances are you are not going to wear that either. Out it goes. "But if I get rid of everything, I'll have nothing to wear!" Guess what—you already had nothing to wear. What's left is all you were actually wearing anyway.

7. Now for the **pile in the other room.** Remind yourself that NOTHING is coming back into your space! NOTHING! Instead **determine ways to give all these things a new life.**
    → Have your friends over and let them just take what they want.

→ Have a yard sale and put the money away for your next shopping trip.

→ Take the winter weather items to a shelter.

→ Sell them through a consignment shop.

→ Donate the whole lot to a charity of your choice—most even take items that are stained or worn and recycle them.

→ None of it needs to be thrown away. Likewise, none of it is a part of your life anymore.

Whew! How do you feel? Better than you thought you would, admit it. You want to know why? Aside from the obvious mental and physical clutter overload that these excess pieces of clothing were creating, they were also wreaking havoc with your self-esteem. I know all too well those feelings of failure when you are desperately trying to find something to wear and nothing fits, trying on piece after piece that is too tight or makes you look like a blob, playing out scenarios in your head about how people will think you've let yourself go. That feeling of self-consciousness and awkwardness, sucking in any body part you can, trying to gloss over your insecurities with banter so no one notices what you look like. (Can you tell I have anxiety issues?) It's exhausting! And depressing. And the worst possible way to motivate anyone to get fit and thin. Incentive clothes DO NOT WORK! Although they do kinda make me want to run... toward a bowl of pasta.

Once you've done the work, your space and head will be free and clear. No need to feel defeated for gaining weight or living in clutter. You've seen the error of your ways and realize you don't have to live with those fashion failures as a constant, guilt-inducing reminder. Nor will you have to hunt through a mountain of closet chaos to find what fits. It's in that joy that you will be motivated to lose weight, if you so wish to be motivated. You are living in the now, where your dresser drawers open and close smoothly because they are not filled with balled-up clothes preventing them from working properly. And the closet, with the floor you hadn't seen in years because of clutter, is now a place filled with clothes that feel custom made for you. What a rush!

Now that you no doubt have a lot less clothes, don't make the mistake of filling your space back up after you've done the hard work of paring down. Don't just go out and shop. Think about what you are really missing, what you really need, what would make you happy to own, and then by all means, go and find it. But don't bring home any "maybe this will work" or "this is good enough" or "it's not quite right but it's on sale" pieces. If you can't find exactly what you're looking for, keep looking. And if you don't need anything, enjoy the space. There is always the option of just living with less.

ADVICE: Do you feel like shopping for a few new seasonal items to spruce up your look but don't want to mess with the perfection of your newly streamlined dream closet? **Give to get!** Collect a bag of castoffs, and drop them at the donation center on your way to the shops. Ideally, one piece out for one piece in, but if you want to be really brave, two for one is the best way to go. It's that easy!

"But wait," you say. "Fit is not my issue. I'm the same size I was in high school." First, I'd reply "Wow, good for you," in as sarcastic a tone as I could muster, followed by a wink and a laugh to let you know I'm just kidding around, and then go on to explain that **this system works the same way for any of your overcrowded wardrobe woes.** Do you have several lifetimes sharing space in your closet? Do you have an abundance of impulse purchases? Do you have drawers of T-shirts from every concert you've ever attended that have more holes than fabric? Or do you just have too much because it's "still good"? I think you know what I'm going to suggest. Purge, purge, and purge some more. At one point I owned more yoga pants than someone who has never actually taken a yoga class before should own. I pared them down to a single-digit collection by returning anything still tagged. Yes, I might eventually use them, but why have my money tied up in spandex when I already had nine pairs in rotation? I wish that were a joke but it's not, so feel free to laugh.

Here are the questions to ask yourself if you just have more clothes than space:

- **Is it in any way damaged—stained, faded, misshapen fasteners, misshapen by wash, etc.?**
- **Does it look good on you?**
- **Do you wear it regularly?**
- **Have you worn it recently?**
- **Is it still tagged after months in your closet?**
- **Do you honestly have any use for it?**
- **Would someone you know get better use out of it?**
- **Did you wear it but no longer need it?**
- **Did you buy it on sale because it was on sale?**
- **Did you forget you had it?**
- **Do you still like it?**
- **Have you read through all of these questions and still are saying "but it's still good"?**

You know what I'm going to say now. If you're not using it, move it along. But hey, this is a book about downsizing clutter. If you have a mansion-sized celebrity closet with a strobe light runway, keep it all! You've got the room. If not, something, excuse me, a lot of things, have to go!

Last point I'd like to reiterate. You've pulled it all out. You've asked yourself the right questions. You've made your piles and sent a good percentage of clothes onto their next adventure. Now you're starting each day with this renewed wardrobe. But you still somehow keep bypassing that yellow button down shirt. It fits, you have reason to wear it, and it's in good condition. But it's not in the rotation. **Either work it onto the team roster or make it a free agent.** We're not keeping things for no good reason anymore. Use it or lose it.

Bottom line, these are clothes. Most of us don't have bespoke designer Met Gala–worthy duds made of archival silk spun by magic fairies. Our clothes came from a store off a rack with thousands of other identical pieces. Letting go of them is not all that difficult precisely for that reason—they are replaceable. What cannot be replaced, however, are physical space in your home, time spent getting dressed, self-respect when you feel unattractive or defeated, and money lost on useless purchases. Please take that all into consideration the next time you say, "But I can't get rid of it" and then promptly return it to the back of the closet with the other clothes you haven't worn in years.

Nothing is more important when it comes to your clothes, or your life for that matter, than feeling comfortable and confident with yourself. Don't punish yourself for growing old, gaining weight, making impulse purchases, or holding onto things past their point of usefulness. Instead, let go of the triggering item, absolve yourself of the error in judgment, and give yourself permission to be who you are now in this moment. I for one am happy to say that after that overhaul, my wardrobe is filled only with clothes perfectly suited to me. Should the need arise for something new, I vow to buy only what fits, is appropriate for the occasion, and makes me look and feel fantastic. Fingers crossed it's also on sale.

2

Little Patrick's Paint Projects Are Not Picassos

Client: "I have kept every arts and crafts project my kids have ever made. I can't just throw them away. You would do that? I could never. I'm guessing you're not sentimental."

BBT: (voice in my head, in my friend Julie's South Carolina accent) *"Bless your heart, darlin."*

One of my very first clients was Rory. She wanted to make over her children's former play and craft room into a more teen-friendly gaming and entertainment space. She was referred to me by a friend of a friend who had given me some insight into what I might be up against with Rory's personality. She said she was not going to be easy to work with, perhaps even belligerent, but her home was magnificent. I accepted the challenge.

Every first impression of the day is still seared in my memory. I can envision the winding driveway that led to her white-washed, all-brick colonial house that sat on a hill surrounded by bonsai-esque trees bordering a perfectly manicured lawn. It was autumn and I whimsically imagined in storybook fashion the trees not daring to drop any of their leaves on the grass for fear of being cut down. (My imagination is quite vivid when I'm overcaffeinated.) In the yard was a treehouse with a rope ladder and a tire swing in a child-sized fairy garden. A gazebo set for a floral tea party completed the scene, which looked like something out of the pages of an intricately staged magazine shoot. Everything was in pristine condition, which made me wonder if any of it had ever actually been used by her children, both of whom were now high schoolers.

Her children, a set of twins, one girl, one boy, had both moved past the age of finger paints and glitter-covered construction paper. These days neither kid was actively involved in anything artistic, but if there was something crayon-covered made by a one-time preschooler, Rory had kept it, boxed and labeled, and stored like the archives of the Smithsonian. In fact, upon seeing the system she was so rightfully proud of, I jokingly asked if there was a card catalog to cross reference and half expected her to produce one.

The playroom hadn't been used in years but it was decorated like the interior of a kindergarten classroom before the school day starts. The aforementioned art collection was stored along one wall in stacked colored plastic bins—pink for Lexi, blue for Daniel—and each stack sat under a hand-painted sign of the child's name in balloons and bubble letters, as if the gender-specific colors were not enough to inform the observer. As far as organizing was concerned, Rory had that covered. But these stacks took up a good portion of the room, space I was going to need to accomplish all the goals she wanted for its new purpose. Convincing her to downsize the museum of kids' crafts was my first hurdle, and I knew that was not going to be an easy sell.

"You're looking at the boxes, aren't you? Don't worry, they're not all full. But don't even think about it 'cause I'm not getting rid of them."

"I haven't said a thing. But yes, we are going to have to do something with them. Besides the fact that they are taking up a lot of space, they are not going to coordinate with your vision for the new room. My suggestion is to downsize and consolidate the contents into a reasonable amount so the rest can be stored someplace else." I was trying to be both compassionate and assertive but I was already rubbing her the wrong way.

"No. They'll work fine here. We can build some cabinets to hide them," Rory said, becoming aggressive.

"Would you at least humor me and show me what's inside?"

Rory took a pink box off the pile, placed it on the table designed in height for a three-year-old, and pushed it over to me. She did the same with a blue box.

"Knock yourself out. I'll go make us some tea."

As I suspected, she had kept everything. Not just the artwork, but schoolwork and even greeting cards they received for birthdays. I wondered to myself, why? What was her motivation in keeping all of this? Some things, yes, but not everything! When she came back with the tea, I had to ask.

"Can I just ask, have you kept everything your children ever touched?" I said laughing so she wasn't put off by my sarcasm.

"Everything they have ever made or worked on from preschool through 6th grade. Then they moved onto middle school and wouldn't show me their work, much less let me touch anything."

"OK. Another question. Do you ever go back and look? Or do the kids? I'm just trying to come up with a plan."

"I do occasionally. Keeping everything is what good mothers do, right? Document their kids' childhood? So they can look back one day and remember the good times."

"Sure, to a reasonable degree. I just think that if we are going to create a room that is more in line with who the kids are now, we have to weed through some things that are no longer 'them.' What I'm saying is that not *everything* is worth holding onto, especially when it interferes with creating a room that is better suited to who they are. Will you consider going through this with me first? I can make the process easy on you."

"I'll think about it."

We drank our tea and moved onto discussing redecorating—hurdle number two. She didn't want to get rid of any of the furniture, just rework it into other places in the house.

"This little-kid furniture is adorable and in such good shape. I'd be happy to sell it for you and put the money toward the room. Items like this sell fast."

"One day I'll have grandkids and I'll use it all again."

"Aren't your kids high school sophomores?" I said with a smile.

"Yeah, but I only really like little kids so I'm planning ahead. Teenagers are terrible. That's just the truth."

WOW! That explained so much. The family dynamic was strained at best. Her kids were growing up. They fought a lot, with her and with each other. And for all their outward perfection and seeming happiness, she was struggling to capture the picture of familial bliss she had dreamed of her whole life. I wasn't at all surprised when she went on and on about the days when they were a young family in their coordinating outfits and camera-ready smiles. She said more than once, without a hint of humor, how she "wished they could stay little forever because now they're just brats." It was not my place to judge, but this woman was not winning any "Mother of the Year" awards, though funnily enough, she did have proudly displayed on the windowsill above the kitchen sink a novelty #1 MOM trophy. I had a sneaking suspicion she bought it for the kids to give to her as a Mother's Day gift.

Even without a degree in psychology it was easy to see that the art projects were a way for her to hold onto a time in her childrens' lives when she was better able to manipulate the photo, and consequently fool herself into believing everything was indeed picture perfect and enviable to others and all she had daydreamed her life to be. Her hope for converting the kids' old playroom into a game room was, in her words, so she could "keep an eye on them" as she rambled on about her lack of trust and their disrespect. I held back offering my two cents. It would not have been heard, much less appreciated. I knew I wasn't in a position to help her fix her family dynamics but what I *could* do was talk her through loosening her grip on the past, and in turn on the overabundance of stuff she was storing—stuff that was preventing her from moving forward and embracing the young adults her kids were becoming. These bins may have been reminders of happier times for her, but unfortunately the fabricated happiness associated was not at all helpful to her long-term relationships with her kids.

Counter to what Rory may have said about good mothers keeping everything, stuff does not make a maternal bond. It can actually be a distraction from the reality of the current emotional conditions in a household to be so beholden to the past. It is certainly a collection of stuff worth a second and third look to curate the most valuable pieces in the bunch, but keeping it all just waters down the importance of those items that are truly special.

* * *

So how then do you decide what is worthy of keeping when you begin to admit to yourself that every fingerpaint doodle from your little artistic geniuses is not a masterpiece worthy of the walls of the Louvre? **Start by separating all pieces by child. If you are unsure of the creator, put it aside to ask them.** In Rory's case, this was not necessary. It was already "perfectly" organized.

Next, **start with just one child's things and inspect each piece by asking the following questions**:

- **Was it created using step-by-step instructions either by a teacher or with a kit?**
  If yes, then it is an assignment completed, not art created. **Put it in the out pile.**
- **Is it a "color in the lines" or "color by numbers" anything?**
  This is not art. **Put it in the out pile.**
- **Does it show particular skills or abstract thinking?**
  This is art. **Put it in the keep pile.**

- **Is your child proud of the piece and able to explain its nuances?**
  This is art. **Keep.**
- **Does it bring you enough joy to hang in your home next to any other piece of art?**
  This is art. **Keep.**
- **Final question: Does your child like it?**
  Yes: keep.
  No: out.

ADVICE: Macaroni pasta creations will crumble and/or attract bugs. It's worthy of a couple months' display on the refrigerator at best before it gets pitched. Harsh but true.

"My mother never kept anything of mine," Rory mused as she leafed through her daughter's half-used Disney Princesses coloring books. "Of course, she never did anything at home with me or my sisters the way I did with my kids. I loved doing these craft projects with them. We had 'snacks and crafts time' every afternoon. Sometimes I'd finish them once the kids got bored but just to get them neat. They had already done an excellent job. They were both considered gifted at an early age."

Did you catch all of those? Oh-so-many things were going through my mind. This client had psychological profiles for all sorts of syndromes. But I was in her home to downsize and decorate, not diagnose. I suggested she keep sorting and stay on track; I really didn't want to lose any momentum now that she had agreed to do this with me.

The next two hours were not easy. The more she went through the boxes the closer she came to tears. She told me she felt a mix of disappointment and frustration because her kids didn't appreciate anything she had done for them. "These kids don't care. They ignore me. When I try to suggest activities for us to do together, they roll their eyes and say I'm trying to control them." Before I could filter myself, the words just tumbled out of my mouth with more attitude than I would have given to a less intense client. "Why don't you just ask *them* what *they* want to do?" She went silent so I quickly added, "Oh shit, did I say that out loud?" with mock embarrassment. Thank God she laughed. "Yeah, I know, but I don't want to play friggin' video games or hear about which girls are doing God knows what with what boys. I've known all of these kids since kindergarten. That would make me sick."

We went back to working. There were more regrets to follow. For starters, the craft kits she'd bought to do with them at home were a source of particular pain. Upon further reflection, she had to admit that she had made most of the projects by herself either because the child didn't want to or worse still, she stopped them from doing the craft altogether because "they weren't doing it right." When the words left her mouth, I saw the clarity in her eyes. She was realizing the mistake she had made all those years ago. This was a personal Pandora's box she was not ready to open. She got up and left the table where we were sitting. A few seconds later I heard her crying from the other room.

I may as well let you know upfront here and now in this book that clutter is almost never about having too much stuff and that downsizing is so much more than just getting rid of it. There is always some emotional component, and once you touch the nerve, the pain is sharp. It's the second-biggest reason people hold onto all their clutter—the fear of facing the emotional baggage—the first reason being never attempting to get rid of it in the first place because it's just too much work.

Here was a stay-at-home mother and wife, living a life that was enviable to many, with anything money could buy, and yet she was only pretending to be happy. To her credit, she had been pretending so well for so long that even she didn't realize how miserable she was. But it was all for show, to prove to others that she had "made it," to make friends and strangers jealous, and to make herself feel like she was the amazing mother her own mother was not. Saving popsicle stick boxes was never going to bring her the happiness she envisioned and it certainly wasn't going to create the bonds with her children she imagined would blossom from those forced, play-filled days to the present. The truth was she had lost touch with her kids the moment they chose not to sit or do or be exactly the way she wanted them to be to suit her picture of perfection. She was living a lie. And keeping all their childhood artwork and school papers gave her, falsely so, the impression that she was a "perfect" mother with "perfect" children who had "perfect" relationships with each other (if she said "perfect" one more time I was going to scream). But she had gotten a bitter taste of reality and I was waiting to see which path her realization would take before continuing to recycle construction paper cut-outs—the path of acceptance, or the path of resistance?

Rory came back into the room. She had fixed her makeup but her eyes were still glassy from crying. "I've made a decision," she said, taking a deep breath. "NOT all of it but I think the majority of it can go." I smiled at her with an understanding look and said, "OK then, let's do it."

She sat across from me in silence as piece after piece was released into the trash can next to her. "You know what? I thought I was going to sit here and be so sad at all the memories these things brought back. Truth is I can't remember a single moment that doesn't make me mad now."

"Mad? Why mad?"

"What a complete waste of time. I did all this work so one day my kids would look back at this stuff and say, 'What a great childhood we had, Mom was the best.' I'm pathetic. And my kids hate me."

"OK, I'm sure that's not true, but yeah, things don't appear warm and fuzzy. Guess what? You still have time to change course. In fact, this is a big first step. Getting rid of the little kid stuff? Creating a space for your kids to be who they are now with their friends? This is telling them 'I like you for who you both are at this moment, not just when you were little. And I want us to be closer by spending time together doing things you want to do.'"

She laughed as she wiped the corner of her eyes. I continued, "There are certainly special ones here. Ones with real meaning. Ones that you and the kids genuinely like. Those are the ones to keep. But as a mother myself and someone you've been generous enough to share this part of yourself with, these coloring book pages were never going to be the make-or-break memories of a happy childhood. Your relationship with your kids is the only thing that can do that."

Rory then did the most surprising thing of our time together. She broke down and sobbed right there surrounded by magic marker drawings of red race cars and houses with spirals of smoke coming out of the chimney. "You know what the worst part of all of this is? Until you came here that never occurred to me at all. What the hell have I been doing? Spending all this time organizing and housing all this crap for what? The idea of them being sweet little kids that loved spending time with their mom? That's not even close to the way it was. I was always yelling trying to make everything look perfect." That word again! "Look, before you got here, I actually thought you were going to be really impressed with how organized I kept these boxes. You kinda ruined it," she said, laughing while blowing her nose. "Ha. You think this is bad, you should see all the baby clothes I have in the attic."

"Well, let's just leave that for another day, shall we," I said, handing her another tissue. "And for what it's worth, I am impressed. With how you organized, not why," I said with a wink.

I let her take a break while I took room measurements and pulled out upholstery samples. When she came back she was energized. Her pace quickened. She saw the real value in some pieces and not others. She kept a few that I suggested she frame and we could use in the new room. There were a few others bound for scrapbooks, and she only fought me over one coloring book page I agreed that she should keep once she told me her son had signed it and it was the first time he wrote his name.

When she was finished she had 12 things total, six for each kid. The true art. The memories of a "perfect" childhood. And the bonus was, we now had room to create the new hangout space she wanted where her kids could have friends over and she "could watch them and be ready when they did something stupid." I didn't respond. I reminded myself I was only there to handle the physical clutter, not the psychological.

Rory and I were clearing up when the kids got home from school, and seeing their childhood artwork strewn on the kitchen table among glossy photos of big screen TVs and sectional sofas evoked the kind of responses she needed to hear as the final goodbye to the kids' crafts.

> Lexi: "Oh, I remember this drawing. You still have that? I can't wait for this room to be finished! I already told everyone we're going to have a party."

> Daniel: "I couldn't stand that art teacher. She made us do the dumbest stuff. Don't forget a cabinet to put all my game stuff in so you don't complain that it's all over the place."

There was clearly more work to be done on the relationships between mother and children, but my work was done as far as the task I was being paid to do. We downsized the old to make room for the new. And as always, my secret hope was that I had also left the family in better shape than I found them.

* * *

Let's recap this process. As in the last chapter, don't start unless you can devote the time to getting it done; otherwise you will have just added to your clutter.

1. **Separate the individual projects by child.**
   If you are unsure who made the artwork in question, put it to the side to ask the creators

directly, unless of course, it goes out based on one of the following questions.

2. **Ask yourself the following for each piece:**
   a. Was it created using instructions? Out pile.
   b. Is it color in the lines or color by numbers? Out pile.
   c. Does it show particular skills or abstract thinking? Keep pile.
   d. Is your child proud of the piece and able to explain it? Keep pile.
   e. Would you hang it in your home as art? Keep pile.
   f. Does your child like it? Yes: keep. No: out.

3. **Store and label by child by school years (pre-school, elementary, middle, high school) in any low-profile (but wide enough) container.** Ideally don't store at all but instead display.

ADVICE: Early on in my organizing career, I would advise clients to **purchase legal-sized document storage boxes**—one per child for each year. Children's art is oftentimes oversized and document boxes are an ideal size for storage purposes (both in terms of width/length but also because their low profile limits how much you can keep). When a box was filled, it was marked "Patrick Age 3," and you were done. Nothing more could be saved without first pitching something else. But I've since changed my advice on this. You shouldn't need to keep nearly that much. The guidelines above should be sufficient to break down the collection by age group instead of by year.

NOTE: Document box storage is only appropriate for temperature-controlled locations like finished indoor closets since the boxes are made of cardboard. You can opt for plastic storage, but ideally **anything worthy of keeping is also worthy of displaying in your home and not stored at all.**

4. **Let your child have the final decision regarding what is saved.** Ultimately, the exercise of saving their childhood creations is for them. Using the guidelines above, **your child is the best candidate to decide what to keep and they should continue to consolidate as time goes by**. When my daughter was about ten, we pulled out her boxes. Afterwards, she had one small box and the best were framed and hung. The rest were recycled or trashed.

NOTE: Just because it's made of paper does not mean it is recyclable. Check your local town or county guidelines for what is acceptable to recycle. Throwing non-recyclable items in with the recycling sadly renders the entire contents trash.

* * *

Remember when Rory suggested that I was "not sentimental"? I'm actually quite sentimental. When it came to my own daughter's artwork, all pieces were immediately and proudly displayed on the refrigerator, the cabinet doors, or the walls, then sorted and either pitched or stored. In anticipation of my aforementioned home sale and her heading off to college, we weeded through what was left of her boxes and were both surprised to find that even we had kept items that did not deserve the space they were taking up. Nearly everything made its way to the garbage or recycling bin that day. The only thing we saved was her handprint-covered preschool graduation cap. How fateful and fortunate that that should be the item we kept, given that the "Quarantine" Class of 2020 did not get a traditional graduation.

My favorite, however, is a piece that I framed almost immediately after she made it, because it was just that special! As soon as she came home from the first day of kindergarten, she sat down with a scrap piece of torn construction paper and crayons and set to work drawing stick figures on stick playground equipment. When she was finished, she explained that she had drawn what recess looked like and that her new classmates were all represented. She told me each of their names and could identify them individually even though there was no distinction between each circle head and line limbs. (At least not to me.) She drew it without prompting, no instructions, no help. Just a whim to draw what she experienced during her first day of school.

That's a keeper. That's art!

ADVICE: These same strategies can be applied in the same way to children's books, toys, and clothes, which can and should be handed down, donated, given away, or consigned/sold. Since the working window for such items is so small in a child's physical and developmental growth, these items rarely outlive their usefulness with just one child. It's important to give them a second, third, or even more extended life. And if you do wish to keep items for sentimental purposes or to pass down to the next generation (my daughter wore the same baptism gown that I myself wore), make sure to choose wisely. Elastic becomes brittle and cracks, snaps rust and discolor surrounding fabric, batteries in toys will corrode. Not everything can be saved.

* * *

As for Rory and her kids, as previously suspected, that tea party under the gossamer fabric canopy was indeed set dressing. The kids never played with it. In fact, it was staged just a few years earlier when the kids certainly had no interest. The only one to ever touch it was the cleaning lady who dusted it. Thankfully, the room that did get its share of wear was the new entertainment room. When it was completed, I even got a few high fives from the kids and their friends, along with a hug and a smile from Rory.

It goes without saying that we as parents are sentimental about all the moments in our children's childhoods. What to keep and what to pitch, though, at some point ultimately comes down to the decision of what to remember, not what to hold onto. Happy memories live in your day-to-day lives as you build them. A healthy childhood is about the bond you forge with your children and the traditions and experiences you share. Yes, certainly you want mementos of the journey—but not at the cost of anything more important.

3

Retail Therapy Is Not as Cute as You Think

Client: "Guess I went a little overboard on the retail therapy. Cheaper than the real thing, am I right?"

BBT: "Ha ha ha. No, not at all!"

It goes something like this. You've got that bored, blah, or even worse, depressed feeling. You feel the need to just get out with a quick trip to Target to buoy your spirits. You promise yourself you'll just pick up laundry detergent and light bulbs, but you come home with throw pillows, yoga pants, and thirty dollars' worth of party supplies for Cinco de Mayo from the clearance aisle. It's an adrenaline rush finding everything you never knew you always wanted in one place AND on sale. But that high is short lived. Once you get home, you realize you don't have any room for more throw pillows, you already have six other pairs of the same yoga pants (two still with tags), and it's May 7th. That's when your new purchases sit in their bags on the periphery of foot traffic for days, weeks, sometimes years if they get stuffed in the corner of a room barely used. You keep telling yourself you'll take them back or you'll give them as gifts or you'll sell them on any of several online marketplaces, but eventually, they will become part of the clutter cycle of "retail therapy."

I've seen it countless times. Sometimes it's an archeological dig of abandoned purchases with price tags and receipts detailing a timeline of low points in a personal history. Much like the euphoria from a drug-induced high, it feels good at the time, but once the effects wear off, you are often left with regret or the compulsion for another spree. Tragically, this type of addiction can be directly linked to credit card debt, bankruptcy, issues in a marriage or business partnership, and increased depression or anxiety. Retail therapy is anything but therapy.

I've said it before, and I will no doubt say it a few more times—I am not a mental health professional. But you don't work in this business for any number of years and not pick up on a few patterns. Retail therapy comes down to one thing—attempting to buy happiness.

* * *

My client Samantha was a case in point. Twice divorced and recently remarried, she and her new husband lived with his daughter and son from a previous marriage and the son they shared. Even though you could barely open the front door to get into the house without swiping a mountain of coats, shoes, and backpacks, there were also shopping bags of purchases—clothes, junk food, makeup, video games, and in one bag, cold groceries going bad. I jokingly but rather bluntly said, "What's going on here? Your mess is already greeting me at the door."

"I know. I know. I'm a mess. I'm so crazy busy trying to get my business up and running while also getting another master's degree. Jack is working long hours too. And the kids' schedules are so full. I'm surprised I remembered to put pants on," she said with a sad laugh.

Had I not seen the despair in her eyes, my first response might have been, "You still managed to find the time to shop," but she was clearly at the end of her rope. The best course of action was compassion as well as a sit-down, where she and I were going to talk about downsizing, organizing, and lifestyle systems, but also shopping habits. Samantha was not the first overshopper I ever worked with and she wasn't going to be the last. Consumerism is an easy, legal fix that is ingrained in us from an early age when we learn shopping is a treat, spending is power, and happiness is in the purchasing and owning of stuff.

I cleared a space between the abandoned dinner plates at her kitchen table, scooted the teacup Chihuahua off the chair, and invited her to join me so we could discuss a plan of action. With the kids all in school and her husband at work, I wanted that time to chat uninterrupted. Somewhere between moving the laundry basket off her seat and tripping over her stepson's baseball cleats, she started to get choked up.

"I know what you're going to say. I do. There's too much stuff. I don't even know what most of it is. I'm stressed and I don't want to be home in this chaos so I go out, and when I'm out, I shop. Believe me, I know how screwed up that sounds."

Her voice cracked the more she told me. From her childhood growing up with a single mother where every penny went to food and heat and rent, to getting a full scholarship to an Ivy League college and wanting to fit in so badly she started to rack up a huge credit card balances, then onto two failed marriages and what she suspected was a third on the way, all of which left her financially strapped. Her only escape and seeming joy was shopping.

She bought the kids the things she never had growing up. She bought the luxuries for herself she couldn't afford early on. She bought into the picture of perfection by having the right clothes and the right car and the right-looking lifestyle all because she believed it would make her happy and undo all the misery and sense of lack she grew up with. But ultimately, it only compounded the problem.

She had convinced herself that she didn't spend extravagantly, always getting the biggest bang for her buck, so that in that regard she was being smart with her money. But the volume and frequency of spending overall and on items of little to no use were her biggest downfalls. The cumulative effects were costing her more than just her financial well-being.

This situation could not be remedied by just separating the mess and putting it in labeled canisters. This was going to take an intervention and full participation of everyone in the house. But first, I had to get through to her that she didn't need to find her bliss in a shopping bag. She already had the makings of a beautiful life, plus enough inventory to open her own Costco.

Often when we are in that vulnerable mindset of "ugh, let's just go shopping" we are not only distracting ourselves from what we don't want to see (everything that's going wrong), but unknowingly also distancing ourselves from what we can't see (everything that's going right). With Samantha, as with other clients before and since, I attempted to get her to see all that was wonderful and worthy about her life, from her multiple college degrees to her budding business to her generous heart. I wanted her to see that when she turned her back on the mess, she was also turning her back on her accomplishments. And the life she had built was part of that list.

I suggested she begin to look at her life as "enough." That there was nothing she could buy that could compare to what she already had. That what she had been doing was looking at her life through the lens of lack instead of abundance. That if she wanted to flip the switch on her perspective, her first step was to look at her clutter as a blessing rather than a curse. And that blessing needed to be treated with respect.

We spent the better part of our time together that day coming up with a plan to systematically, room by room, strip and reorganize her home. But we also laid the groundwork for a new way of thinking, one I hoped would stop this cycle of binge shopping from happening again and thus undoing all the hard-fought efforts put in place. Because when it comes to retail therapy, downsizing is twofold—paring down what you already have and preventing more from coming in. Those steps have to take place in tandem or slipping back into old patterns is inevitable.

NOTE: Downsizing is NOT something I do alone. I work alongside the client. It is not up to me to decide what stays and what goes. I'm there to give guidance, ask tough questions, and facilitate the movement, removal, and momentum of the task at hand. It's also during this often intense process that I learn what I need to know about the client's habits, family dynamics, and lifestyle for when I will be organizing the space afterwards.

Step 1 is **downsizing what has already been purchased.** The positive in downsizing the retail therapy loop is that in general, the mindset of this shopper has little to do with the products being purchased. It's the act of purchasing that holds the thrill. What that means is that most of what is sitting around as clutter is unused and still tagged. It is easy to identify and return to the store for a refund or store credit, assuming it has not gone too far past the return date. If that's the case, it's still new so it can be easily sold or gifted. What that also means is that since the "high was in the buy," there is less attachment to the products bought. Less attachment equals easier to let go... conceivably.

I told you about the clutter that met me at the door of Samantha's house. With the exception of the food, I told her it should all go back. Every item was an impulse purchase and she didn't need any of it. She tried to make the case for them because she had gotten everything for a deep discount.

"All of that was on super sale. I can always use a white blouse. And the lipstick is a fun new color I thought might be nice to try. And the video game is for my son who finally got his math grade up. No, those are all good purchases."

"OK, here is where I change your mind about how to buy. Can you use a white blouse? Let me rephrase. WILL you use THIS white blouse? I mean, how many white blouses do you already own and how often do you wear them?" I asked with a raised eyebrow in a joking tone. "And," I said, pulling the lipstick from the bag, "I guarantee that once we clear through this house, you will find no fewer than five, maybe ten, unopened new colors of lipstick." Then getting more serious, "And lastly, this is just the mommy in me talking and I'm trying to say this in the kindest way possible, but you've mentioned your son's math grades before. I think buying him a video game is sending him the wrong message about how to spend his time. Why not have his reward be choosing where you all go for dinner or what to do together on the weekend? Then you get the benefit of family time without the gaming distraction from his study time."

I knew I hit a nerve, but tough love is tough. She reluctantly agreed that because she was fully committed to this process of getting her home and life in order, that these things could go back to the store. I made it easier on her by saying I would do all the returns for her. The truth was, I didn't think she'd follow through so I took the matter into my own hands. Goodness knows it takes more than one afternoon of me pilfering through shopping bags for a client to see the benefits of all these new changes to their lifestyle habits and I couldn't risk at this point her just hiding those bags in her car. To break the habit of impulse buying, everything had to go **back to the store, both freeing space and reimbursing finances.** My fingers were crossed that these rewards would prove to be better highs than shopping.

Retail Therapy Is Not as Cute as You Think

So, phase 1 of step 1 is to break the retail therapy hold by **returning anything and everything that can be returned—ideally for a refund but at the very least for store credit.** It should be easy enough to find what goes back... the still-tagged items are more than likely in the original shopping bags with the receipt.

NOTE: Don't have the receipt but know where you bought it? Some stores can trace your purchase with the debit or credit card you used; no need for a receipt so no excuse to keep it. Regardless, it never hurts to ask.

Phase 2 of step 1 is to **divide and conquer but pick your battles.** I should warn you now, depending on the extent of the shopping habit, this could easily be weeks of work. Be methodical. Be focused. And only bite off what you can chew in a given amount of time. The idea is to build momentum. Don't start with the largest room in the house. **Start with the smallest, finish it, and take a break.** Let the feeling of accomplishment push you onward.

In Samanatha's house we started in the foyer. The bags of new purchases were already in my car to be returned and the groceries were quickly put away in the kitchen. Next step, **everything gets sorted and moved to temporary locations.**

Have you ever seen one of those plastic "goody" bag games where you move the tiles around a board until they create a picture? That's this step. Items get moved

49

but may not stay where they are placed as things get shuffled around to create a space. The goal is to **keep moving through each space, sorting and clearing what doesn't belong, and for the moment, just putting things in the appropriate room, not necessarily in their final place**. In the foyer we collected shoes, sports equipment, book bags, and any other extraneous personal items and put them into the room of the appropriate family member. Yes, many of those items would be coming back into the foyer/mudroom, but not all. I didn't want her to waste any time at this point deciding what stayed or went when we were in the midst of bulldozing the area. Time enough for that step once we got to that room. We did the same in tackling the living and dining rooms. Why these spaces first? Because they had less clutter, were easier to clear, and helped to get Samantha in the momentum mindset she needed to continue after I left for the day.

ADVICE: Use large plastic bins—yes, I said bins—to sort items as you move through each space. Once filled, bring that box to the appropriate room in one go instead of running back and forth with just an armful of items.

Even though those first three rooms were completed in less than a day, it would take us the next full week to purge the main spaces of the house—family room, kitchen, and master bedroom. From morning until late afternoon each day, she and I methodically sorted through each space, finding more items that could be returned, other things that could be trashed, and a bunch of stuff that fell into the categories of donate, gift, or use. Oh, and not to say I told her so, but once the master bedroom was completed, we had indeed found multiple unused lipsticks, one in fact the same shade she had just bought. We both got a good laugh out of that one.

* * *

For the purposes of laying out how best to approach any room that is teeming with overpurchasing, basic clutter, and messiness, **here's your plan of attack.**

1. **Gather bins for sorting items into categories, boxes for packing up items for donation, shopping bags for returns, garbage bags for the obvious.**

2. **Do a quick run-through of the room to collect trash, dirty plates, etc., that are easy to spot.**

3. **Clear a working surface for a sorting area. For example, in a bedroom, make the bed and lay a sheet down on top for this purpose.**

4. **Start in one section of the room and work**

your way around, ultimately working yourself and the boxes out of the door. I like to work through a room clockwise but find the system that makes sense for you.

5. **Have a bin just for the new items that still have tags on them. As it fills up, so do the dollars potentially refunded. Likewise, it's a good test to see how much you have spent on items you haven't used. Hold onto that feeling for a moment. It's regret, and it's not something you want to feel again.**

6. **Sort items into categories. (For example, some of the categories in a bathroom might be towels/linens, makeup/toiletries, and backup supplies.) From there, determine what gets returned, what gets trashed, what goes to donation, and what you keep. Bear in mind always that what is kept will have to be organized into the space. Keep only what you are currently using or what you will use in the near future.** Here's a quick trick you can literally do with anything you own en masse. Gather the items all together side by side. You'll be surprised to discover that you really don't love them all once you see them in comparison to each other. Your favorites will stand out from the pack. Keep those, and let the rest go.

NOTE: I do believe in an appropriate number of backup supplies (soap, toothpaste, toilet paper, for example). By all means be ready for when you run out of what you are currently using. But if you use a new shampoo and after that first use you can't stand the fragrance on your head all day, your chances of ever washing with it again are slim to none. Get rid of it. Most charity dropoff locations will take partially used toiletries (check on their website). Maybe give the item to a friend. Don't let it take up space in your home.

7. **At the end of each day, remove everything you've accumulated and put it in your car. Return as much tagged merchandise as possible as soon as possible. Drop off any donations immediately. Take trash to the dump if you are a week away from garbage day. The point is to clear out these items quickly so you won't risk bringing them back into the house. You can see the benefit of the process and that realization will help you immensely during phase 2.**

8. **Remember that you have options here: return, donate, gift, sell, trash. Note that none of those options is keep. You have enough!**

Which brings us to step 2: **breaking the habit of retail therapy by learning your shopping personality.**

SECRETS TO YOUR SPENDING TRIGGERS

<u>Shopper personality #1:</u> Do you have a penchant for one or more specific items? Samantha was surprised to discover she had a thing for makeup, especially lipstick. I myself have been known to overdo it on office supplies (I never said I was perfect). **If this is the case, learn to shop your stock.**

→ **Gather that one collection of items from all around your house.**

→ **Downsize each assortment using part of the criteria from Chapter 1:**

> **Does it fit or work for your needs and lifestyle?** For example: once my daughter started using college ruled notebook paper, there was no need for wide ruled. I donated it to her school to be used for the younger grades.

> **Is it in good or usable condition?** I collected the pens from all over the house and tested them—if you don't test them, you are definitely holding onto trash. I bagged a bunch to donate—you can literally donate anything usable. I then placed what I kept back in their appropriate locations, and designated a drawer in my mudroom for backup supplies.

Do you still like it? Are you likely to use it?
In my case, it was eye opening to see just how many crayons an only-child household could collect over the years. We kept a single assortment for when my little nephews visited and donated the rest.

Answer NO to any of these questions and it goes out. Once you have pared down to what you are using plus a reasonable backstock, you should clearly see there is no value in buying more until necessary.

→ **Separate what you use daily from your backstock.** Organize the rest of your backstock in one easy-to-access place so when you've used up your current supply and need more, you can **shop your stock.** Believe me, it has the same feel as shopping—which if we're truth telling, you've already done. You just won't be spending any money!

Shopper personality #2: Maybe your go-to buy is not specific to one category but a longing to improve yourself in some way. Be it sports or crafts or travel, do you have items you bought that you planned to use at some point? Like maybe those skeins of yarn you bought when you decided to learn to knit? Or the yoga mat that hasn't been unrolled? Or that new set of luggage for that someday European holiday? No time like the present. **That "use it or lose it" moment has arrived!**

Much like with the idea of "incentive clothes" in Chapter 1, these items are not providing you with any motivation. Instead they are a constant reminder that you spent money on something you ultimately didn't use with the hopes of gaining a new experience that you ultimately didn't have. That's not an incentive, that's a detriment. It's a reminder of yet another expense for yet another lack of better judgment. Word to the wise: **do not buy it until you are going to use it.**

Shopper personality #3: This one, on many levels, is by far the worst of the three—the thrill of the bargain hunt that fuels the shopping habit. Do you find something, anything, at a great price and think, "I can't pass this up. They are practically giving it away"?

This one is the hardest of the habits to break because it is the most emotionally fueled. This kind of shopper will pick up a medium-sized chartreuse see-through men's dress shirt, literally not knowing a soul who can or will wear it, see that it's only $5.00, and then buy TWO! Why?!

Because it fills a void. It feeds an aching. It presents the shopper with the luxury to purchase without consideration of cost or practical thought, which makes them feel rich, frivolous, and unburdened by reasonable responsibility. The fact that it is purchased with the thought of not keeping it for themselves but in giving it to someone else makes them feel generous. And all those emotions make them feel important and perhaps even a bit powerful. Bet you never considered that all those nuances were wrapped up in the buying of that tacky piece of clothing that will never be worn. Those nuances, however, are exactly why it is so difficult for this shopper to stop.

Thankfully, I have seen **success in talking clients through this using the following advice:**

→ **Stay out of stores as much as possible.** Don't tempt yourself.

→ **Shop your stock before you shop the store.** It feels just as good.

→ **Do not browse until you have mastered not buying.** In fact, don't even do it then.

→ **Shop with a list and stick to it.** If it's not on the list, you don't need it.

→ **Don't buy unless there is an imminent need/ use.** Otherwise you're overbuying.

→ **Remind yourself of the huge amount of tagged merchandise you collected from around your house earlier while downsizing.** It was far more than you expected, wasn't it?

→ **More importantly, remind yourself of the hundreds, if not thousands, of dollars spent on products that served no purpose other than to collect dust.** Ugh! That one makes me sick thinking about it.

→ **Instead, try borrowing or bartering before you buy again.** Think about that the next time you need a dress for your coworker's daughter's wedding and you have a friend your same size.

→ **And finally, find ways to cultivate those same feelings of importance by giving gifts of your time and talents.** Your grown son doesn't want a novelty light-up naked Santa's helper tie even if it only costs you a buck, but he might appreciate you watching the grandkids so he can take his wife to dinner.

When I have clients that fall into this last personality, I know I'm going to be in for a fight. To them, my insistence that they get rid of things AND curb their shopping feels like I'm robbing them of happiness. Nothing could be further from the truth. Overshopping only *feels* like happiness, and only at first. Then it feels like regret, anxiety, and abandonment. But to the mind of the overshopper, it's not the purchasing that is to blame for these feelings, but the lack of more.

And there it is! Lack. The lack of possessions is not the catalyst for the negative moods, emotions, or energy. It's a lack of perspective. **Instead of viewing your life as missing everything you don't have and still need, switch that perspective to appreciating all you do have and don't need.** No, really—try. I'll give you an example to help flip the switch.

Say your favorite department store is having a white sale—50% off those expensive designer sheets with the outrageous thread count that puts you to sleep just thinking about them. With a mindset of lack and need, you'd get in the car immediately and buy two of everything since of course, at 50% off, it's the same as two for one. But with a mindset of abundance and gratitude, you might not even notice the advertisement because it wasn't on your radar. And even if you did notice, you might think, "That's a great price, but I've got enough sheets that are in perfectly good condition so I'm good, besides, I've been sleeping so well these days because life is going so well because I'm completely content and grateful for my beautifully abundant life, I don't need the luxury of that threadcount to get me to sleep." OK, maybe that's a bit over the top, but it's not that far off from the emotion of this very scenario.

Let's look at this another way. No one likes to feel hungry, but as a biological survival response it lets our brains know that our bodies need food. A negative reaction to needing sustenance produces a positive action by alerting us it's time to feed the body. Oddly enough, acquiring things feeds a similar emotional response, except that shopping is not a need. Owning things is not necessary to survival. Acquisitions are purely desire based. It's a fact that no one enjoys the feeling of want or lack. When your perspective on your life is that you don't have enough or what you have is not good enough, the triggering reaction feels like a need to acquire more and "better" things. Unlike eating, though, once you've made the purchase to fill the void, you're still hungry. Why? Because it's not items that fix this kind of need. It's self-love, acceptance, gratitude, and well-being. Those can't be bought for any price. The feeling of having enough of everything or that everything you have is more than good enough breeds contentment and happiness.

Try this. Look around any room in your house. If there is anything that gives you an "off" feeling, get rid of it. Tags or not. Recently purchased or not. On sale or not. Now look again. Is there anything that makes you literally smile or just lightens your mood? Add that item to the mental tally sheet of things that are good in your life. The goal, of course, is to clear what feels wrong and embrace what feels right. Tip the scales in your favor and you know what you get? A life that feels really full of positives instead of stuff.

* * *

Retail therapy is not therapeutic when it adds to your clutter, depletes your bank account, creates distance both physically and emotionally from your relationships, and does not fill a void of unhappiness because it's actually causing it. Remember at the start of this chapter, in the conversation with my client, when she said, speaking of retail therapy, "Cheaper than the real thing"? Indeed it is not!

Stop shopping the clearance aisle attempting to buy happiness and instead find a good therapist to help you discover the happiness within. Their fees will cost you far less in the long run and unless they've opened a new department I'm unaware of you won't find their offices at Target, so there's no chance you'll happen upon any items you just can't pass up in the process.

4

Preserve Gramma's Legacy, Not Her Toilet Paper Cozy

Client: "It's so nice to finally meet you face to face. I can't thank you enough for all the advice you gave me as I cleaned out my great aunt's house. I think I did a pretty good job getting rid of most of it, but this stuff!" (shaking her head and pointing to her garage full of boxes) *"Every time I start to go through it I just wind up doing nothing. I'm in over my head with this stuff!"* (panic rising)

BBT: "It's OK. No worries. We're going to take this slow and steady, keeping in mind always what will best honor her memory while serving you as well."

I can certainly appreciate what a very personal and emotion-filled situation it is to have to clear out the home of a loved one who has passed. I have been witness to the tears and regrets and obligations these belongings can provoke in people who are grieving. It is an unfortunate but intimate byproduct of being in home organizing. And because of it, I find it is in everyone's best interest that I let the client take the lead. I view my job solely as a calming voice of reason sprinkled with a bit of comedic relief for when things get a little intense.

- "I can't just let it go!"
- "It was expensive."
- "It's antique."
- "It's collectible."
- "It's an heirloom."
- "It's been in the family for years."
- "It was hers."

Common and reasonable explanations all. But if you don't like, want, or have room for whatever it is, then does it really honor your loved one in any way by being a burden to you? I know some of you are itching right now to prove to me that your great grandmother's porcelain pig collection is worth thousands even though you will never let it see the light of day, or that your great uncle's crystal candy dish with the dusty Jordan almonds still in it holds some sentimentality even though you never met him. And before you call me names, I realize how unsympathetic I sound. But please hear me out. I am not being disrespectful of your feelings or the love you shared with this person or who they were, which was no doubt impactful. I am attempting to break through the sense of faux nostalgia that is preventing you from letting go of things you actually don't want but think you need to keep.

Here's the truth. I'd hate to think that one day my future granddaughter will be holding onto a coffee mug I owned just because it was in my house when I passed. Not my favorite mug or one that I used to serve her hot cocoa in when she came to visit. Not even one that matches the set she has at home. Not a fit for her in any way other than that it was in my cabinet after I died. No, I in fact do NOT want her to hold onto it if she doesn't want it. I want her to give it away and in all honesty, that would please me to no end. And why is that, you ask? Because that mug held no special meaning for me. I've got mugs in my cabinet right now that I guarantee could go missing and I wouldn't even notice. Why should anyone keep them out of some sense of sentimentality? Unless, like I said, they happen to need a coffee mug.

I don't have an actual tally but I'm willing to bet that close to 75% of the stuff left behind by a loved one is not worthy of the cardboard boxes they will be packed in. If you're a DAR member, I may stand corrected; let's drop that down to 50%, because even then you know you don't want all those handmade lace doilies in your house. The average American home does not have a significant amount of monetarily or even sentimentally worthy pieces in it. Think about that for a second. That includes, if you are truly being honest with yourself, your beloved family member's homeful of stuff. And she knew it too, or she should have. So unless she said otherwise, she did not expect you to keep it all.

I'd like to ask you this. Were you to die right now, would you, hand to God, expect your family to keep everything you have in your house? I can tell you without a doubt, there are things in my house right now that even I don't want. So, no, I would not expect everything to be kept. Let's be very practical here because this, after all, is what this book is about. We are talking about THINGS, not the memories of the people who owned them. You can indeed let go of the things without letting go of the people or the memories. They ARE mutually exclusive.

* * *

Let me tell you the story of my client at the top of this chapter and maybe that will make what I'm saying seem less judgmental, because of all the clients I've worked with to downsize a home after someone passed, she's the one who took my advice and embraced it, and didn't once question that what I was telling her was in her best interest or the best way of preserving the memory of her dear great aunt.

Eva was an only child of an only child and the last remaining adult member on her father's side. She and her husband and their three children lived in Maryland but her family was originally from Ohio, which is where this great aunt lived. She hadn't seen her in years but they were very close; her great aunt was more like a grandmother to her. The house her great aunt lived in was a long-term rental and the landlord gave Eva as much flexibility as she needed to clear it out, as long as she had it empty in about six months.

A mutual friend had suggested Eva call me for advice on how best to handle the situation and I was happy to offer some help from afar. Before the first of what would be three weekend trips back and forth to Ohio, I suggested she **rent a 16' portable storage container** and have it delivered to her great aunt's driveway. This would not only act as a sorting station while she emptied each room, but would make the process of shipping items back to Maryland that much easier. What I did not tell her then was that it would also limit the amount she could bring home and make choosing wisely all the more important.

It is vital to **have contacts lined up** during a large-scale downsizing. The above-mentioned **portable storage container company** is a case in point. Shop around, especially if you know you will be renting it for a few months and then having it shipped across states. Also, speak with **local organizations that will pick up your donations,** whether furniture or clothes. Having the items picked up helps you remain focused on the task at hand without interruption. Also check with them as some will not take certain items and you will want to know this ahead of time. Lastly, contact the **municipality for trash pickup of large items (like mattresses)** so you can coordinate their removal as well.

I sent Eva the following **to-do list to get herself started** with her first trip to start clearing out the house:

1. **Throw out the contents of the refrigerator and donate any unexpired food from the pantry.**

2. **Collect all your great aunt's clothes, shoes, etc.; choose perhaps a few items that you want to keep for yourself and donate the rest to charity. Collect higher value personal items like jewelry, furs, etc., and pack them with the things coming back with you so you can have them professionally appraised later.**

3. **Bring everything from the basement up and put it directly in the portable storage container. Do not sort at this point. Sorting through boxes now will only be a time sucker from getting the house cleared out.**

In this case, Eva had already told me that the basement was unfinished and there was no furniture downstairs, only boxes. Eva told me later that day that while the boxes weren't heavy they were cumbersome, so **she enlisted the help** of the teen boys next door for a small fee and pizza. She also noted that given the amount of accumulated dust on top, these boxes had not been touched in years.

4. **Lastly, sweep the basement, double-check nothing was left behind, wash out the refrigerator and pantry, put out the trash and donations for pickup, and then take a break to just be in your great aunt's house and reflect.**

ADVICE: Going through the belongings of someone who has passed is an emotional experience, and the closer you were to the deceased, the harder that experience will be. Be focused while working, but also take the time to remember those special moments you shared that marked your lives together. Be kind to yourself during this process. Cry, scream, go for a walk, take an ice cream break, whatever your grief looks like for you while you are in the thick of things, do it. Then jump back in.

5. **One last thing before heading home; please walk through the house and take photos of each room, closet, and cabinet. That way you and I can strategize for your next trip out. Good luck! I'm sure you'll do a great job! Safe travels home!**

On her drive back, she told me she had followed my instructions to the letter with the exception of bringing the jewelry home with her instead of putting it in the storage container and that unfortunately, there were no furs.

She made her second trip about a month later. The house was a single-level, three-bedroom, ranch-style house. Since her great aunt lived alone, only one bedroom was set up for living. The other two bedrooms predictably housed floor to ceiling boxes. I suggested she put her energies into **moving the boxes from these rooms to the storage container.** Remembering my instructions from the first trip, she **scheduled a local thrift shop willing to pick up the rest of the furniture from inside the house** without her having to move it outside. She hated letting it go but she didn't have any need for it or a place to store it at home. **Nor was it particularly fine furniture, so she didn't bother contacting any antique dealers to assess.** She kept just a mirror, a lamp, and one dresser, all of which she knew she would use. Later when she told me this part of the story, I commended her for her critical editing choices and not letting a false sense of obligation force her into bringing it all back to Maryland. And that she should be happy in the knowledge that it would eventually go to a good home while making some money for a good cause.

Trip three did not go quite as well. With her over-booked schedule at home she was trying to make this her last trip to Ohio. The weather was terrible. She had reached the point inside where she felt like either throwing it all away or blindly packing it all up to deal with at some future date back home. The storage container was nearly full and she still had no idea what was in all those boxes. She was feeling in over her head and that was when she called me at the end of her rope.

I told her again that the boxes would be a black hole sucking her time and focus and were best left until last. Especially given the thunderstorm I could hear on the other end of the phone. I explained that as difficult as it would be, she had to be methodical with the remaining things in the house. I asked her to take a break, get something to eat, hydrate, and give me 30 minutes. I would text her a plan.

ADVICE: When you are involved in any purging process, it can be draining. If you are losing steam, take it as a sign to slow down and appreciate what you have accomplished in getting to this place. You are freeing yourself from clutter! Let it give you a second wind to keep going.

Here is my text:

OK, Eva. **Let's take these in order:**

1. **Schedule a donation pickup for the rest of your great aunt's things for the evening**

before the day you are leaving so you are certain it was picked up.

2. Schedule the storage container movers to pick up the portable unit a few days after you head home so you can get a head start.

3. Check that the basement and bedrooms are empty and close the doors.

4. Clear the bathrooms and linen closets. Be certain to dispose of all medication in an appropriate manner (check local guidelines). Decide what you would like to take with you, pack it, and put it immediately in your car.

5. Box/bag the remainder for donation and place it at the designated pickup location.

6. Clear the kitchen and laundry area. Remove everything from cabinets onto the counter so you can assess everything at a glance. Same as above: decide what you would like to take home, pack it up, and put it in your car immediately. Box/bag the remainder for donation and place it at the designated pickup location.

7. Clear the family room. Since you have

already donated the bulk of the furniture, take a second look at what is left behind. As with the other rooms, decide what you would like to take home, pack it, and place it immediately in your car or the storage container. Box/bag the remainder for donation.

8. **Same thing in the living room and dining room as well as any extra closets.**

9. **If you cannot make a clear decision to keep or purge, keep it for now. Keep all paperwork, photos, money, jewelry, documents, and anything with a high perceived value (like china; original, numbered, or signed art; and books) but use your best judgment. It is not practical to bring it all back.**

Call me if you need some help. You've got this. You're nearly there.

Your great aunt would be so happy with the way you're handling this situation.

Thankfully the house was not that big, so with her game plan set, she was remotivated to jump back in. She stayed an extra couple days to get it all done, **and right before she left, did a quick sweep of the now-vacant house to confirm it was clear.**

But telling you this whole story only brings you to Act 2, which is a garage full of boxes, bins, and bags that have yet to be opened back in Maryland, and all of it preventing any cars from being parked inside.

Tackling this situation would take the help of both Eva and her husband Paul, plus my lead assistant, Jesse. There were a lot of boxes. And because any project like this is both physically harsh and emotionally charged, staying focused was critical. Knowing this, Eva thought it best to arrange for the kids to stay with friends for a few days.

I **rented a small outdoor pop-up canopy** to cover the driveway in the event of inclement weather so we could continue to use this space for sorting. **We set up folding tables and lined them with clear plastic bins**—I know, again with the bins—**to sort items by category. We also assembled several cardboard boxes to pack items that would be dropped off at Goodwill at the end of each day. Lastly, we lined trash cans and recycling bins ready for anything being immediately thrown away.**

Jumping right in, we each grabbed a box, opened it, and began **sorting the contents based on what was inside**. About three boxes in for each of us, we had hit a nice stride.

→ **Paperwork went into one bin** (junk mail, circulars, and extraneous envelopes were recycled right away).

→ **Photos went into one bin** (any photo frames were removed, since most of them were not particularly attractive, and trashed or boxed for donation).

→ **Kitchen items were sorted** (Eva kept only what she needed and the rest got boxed for donation).

→ **Clothes were sorted** (again, she kept only what she knew she would wear and the rest went out).

Then things got a bit more difficult as we unboxed things like china, crystal, and silver. **I told her to ask herself the following questions:**

- **Do you like it?**
- **Will you use it?**
- **If not, will you at least display it in your home?**
- **If not, do you know someone who would say yes to any or all of those questions?**
- **If not, are you willing to take the time to research its value and sell it?**
- **If not, would you let me donate these items to an upscale resale shop where they would get the most interest and you'd get the tax writeoff?**

At the end of this quiz, where I fired off these questions in rapid succession, she kept the china (service for 12) and a few crystal vases, but let all of the silver go. Wise choice... silver is a pain in the butt to keep clean.

We were going at a pretty good pace until we hit the Christmas decorations so we decided to wrap up for the day and start fresh in the morning. Jesse took **all the donations to the dropoff center** on her way home. I helped Eva and Paul bring everything they decided they wanted to keep back into the house. I told Eva that if she was up to it, to **wash the china tonight and think about where she might want to display it. Maybe even use it for dinner**... which she told me the next day, they had.

When we started again in the morning we **gathered some packing paper and clean bins**, because any of the Christmas decorations she would decide to keep would have to be stored again—only this time for her own collection. We set up **four boxes to sort into categories—keep, gift, sell, donate.**

NOTE: On the subject of collectible ornaments, yes, there is some value to them; Christopher Radko and Hallmark are two that come to mind. The monetary value varies greatly based on original packaging, condition, and marketplace interest. But think very carefully about the value of any time spent in researching and selling. There are several options; if you really like them, by all means keep some or all. If you'd like to sell them, you can do it on your own through a site like eBay, or sell the collection you have to a collectible site like Replacements, or consign them with an appropriate consignment shop. And then there is always donation. A bit of research will help you decide which process works best for you based on what inventory you have.

Eva was struggling with the right thing to do with all these holiday decorations that clearly her great aunt had taken great interest in collecting. She was rightfully concerned when she said, "I don't want anything we keep to just become clutter here," but she also felt odd just dropping it all off at a donation center. In the end I suggested instead that she keep the ones she immediately liked and hold back the rest for her annual Christmas party with her moms group (an event I knew about because our mutual friend was always a guest). Brainstorming some ideas, I suggested she could lay them all out and her guests could take what they wanted, either for themselves or to gift to someone else. Anything left over she would feel more comfortable donating since she had done her part to give most of them good homes. It turned out to be a fun spin on purging that I have since suggested to a number of clients and that works with anything from hats to hardware. She loved the idea and we got back to work.

The next day, we **set up our work station again and started the next phase of pulling boxes out of the garage.** Until this point, we were handling only the boxes that were in the bedrooms of the house. Now we had gotten to the dust-covered boxes that were previously in the basement. **Donning N95 masks**, which in precoronavirus days were far easier to come by, we started opening them up. We had no idea what we would find. And we were stunned!

There were 27 boxes in total, ranging in size from book boxes to large wardrobe boxes. There was a strong scent of mildew and some staining on the bottom of the nine wardrobe boxes, suggesting water damage. As we carefully opened up the tops, we could see that the boxes contained a mishmash of bedding, towels, pillows, and seasonal clothes, and that unfortunately all of the contents were pretty much destroyed by mold and mildew. For health reasons, we thought it best not to venture further and instead wrapped each box with large plastic construction bin liners and put them out for garbage pickup.

Eva was so frustrated with herself for having brought them back home at all; she assumed the odor was just the lingering smell of the basement and not the boxes. And since she'd had no idea what would be inside, she hadn't wanted to discard anything of value. I assured her there was no crime in doing what she did, and if there was anyone to be frustrated with it was me for telling her to not waste time dealing with them while she was clearing out the house. She laughed and we moved on. The end was in sight.

No one could have predicted what would come next. I still can't believe it myself; it was both shocking and magical. Each of the remaining 18 boxes contained roughly the same assortment of things—collectible souvenir tourist knicknacks. Miniature spoons and thimbles, shot glasses and ashtrays, paperweights, keychains, magnets, trinket dishes, all new in their original packaging, from towns and cities all over the United States. And all of them carefully and individually wrapped in tissue paper.

I turned to her and said, completely stunned, "Does any of this make sense to you?"

"Actually it does," she said, laughing. "It's a great family story. Something about Great Aunt Mary dating a man who traveled for work. I think he sold business insurance. Anyway, she would go with him when he traveled even though they weren't married. My grandmother hated him because he never proposed to her sister but Aunt Mary loved him and they were together for 40 years. Anyway, the only thing I guess is that she bought these from every place they went. My God! This is outrageous!"

We decided to take a little break to figure out our next steps and sat at her kitchen table over coffee to brainstorm how to proceed. If nothing else, going through these items would at least be entertaining. **We discussed the possible options**:

- → **Donate all of it.**
- → **Try to consign or sell it.**
- → **Give it to someone who may be interested.**

- → **Gift it to a museum like the Smithsonian's National Museum of American History (a suggestion from my daughter).**
- → **And then there was always keeping it— either displayed (a near requirement of mine if you are keeping collectibles, otherwise, what is the point?) or boxed (which I felt was allowable in this instance given the personal historic value of how she came by them).**

We landed on a combination of things. She decided she would never use most of this stuff and definitely did not want to display it. That meant everything was marked to go out for donation with the exception of the spoons (she assured me she had her reasons) and the ashtrays (which she planned to set out every time Paul had his buddies over to play cards and smoke cigars in the backyard). From the spoons, we sorted out any that were not food safe and added those to the donations. She had yet to tell me what her idea was, but I could see the wheels turning and her eyes brighten as she got more excited about it.

NOTE: This will come up again in the chapter on collectibles but I feel very strongly that anything that is collected, either by you personally or someone you have inherited from, be USED either practically or for display purposes! Not stored away in preserved boxes to maintain their "value." If that's the case, just sell them off. **Use 'em or lose 'em.**

As we sorted the boxes, Eva told me her idea. Since she entertained on a regular basis, she was going to use the spoons for an apps & desserts tasting party she was planning for the holidays. I thought that was a great idea and added that the spoons would certainly give her and her guests something to talk about as they mused over the exploits of her great aunt.

Then she lit up! I love the excitement in someone's whole person when they get an idea that they just love. She thought out loud, "Wait! I've got another idea. Most of the people who collect these spoons are older folks, right? Assisted living residents. Now bear with me as I talk this through." She was so keyed up, I couldn't wait to hear what she had to say. "So my moms group does an afternoon tea once a month at Sunrise Village. We bring desserts and the kids. The residents get such a kick out of watching the kids play. Well, what if we bring the spoons to use for the desserts, and maybe they can tell us about the places they have been, if any, and then they can keep them?!"

I gave her a huge hug. These are the moments when I absolutely love my job. Not only had she done a phenomenal job during all her back and forth to Ohio to downsize and clean out her great aunt's house, but she was steadfast and focused while going through the boxes back home, making sure to keep only those

things that meant something to her either sentimentally or practically. And now she'd **found a powerful
way to remember her great aunt while spreading joy
to those who would appreciate her things the most.
Not keeping items that she didn't want, boxed away
taking up room just because. But in finding a way to
give these items new life.** We were both so energized
by the way everything played out. We boxed up the
castoffs and I put them in my car to drop at the thrift
store. We were finally done!

I wanted to end our time together on a high note,
so I said that because the few boxes that were still left
were filled with photos, which we could save them
for another time, maybe in a few weeks. And that in
the meantime, she should just go through them and
enjoy the hodgepodge of several decades of fashion
and family, bringing in the kids on the fun of looking
at old photos.

NOTE: Regarding personal paperwork: for security
purposes, I do not handle paperwork but rather give
my clients referrals to services near them that handle
personal and estate paperwork, as well as to local
shredding services in case that's something they need
down the line.

As we pulled down the tent and collected the last
of the trash, she said she was so looking forward to
having the tasting party later in the year and that I had

to promise to attend. I told her I wouldn't miss it for anything... and what a delicious and hilarious time it turned out to be! The incredible menu was rivaled only by the entertainment she'd planned. One by one each guest pulled a spoon from a bag and had to come up with a story. A story of a random US town, of souvenir tchotchkes, cross-country travels, and a lifelong love affair. Then we all raised our spoons in memory of Great Aunt Mary. It was a truly wonderful way to honor her legacy.

* * *

I leave you with this. I have to believe that our loved ones who pass want only to be remembered in the most beautiful way. And if that way is through a special possession, then by all means, hold onto it and use it and cherish it. But no one would want to be remembered for the burden left behind by boxes of unwanted clutter, so pare down your own belongings at least annually. That way, you won't leave anything to your heirs but the best of you. As for the items left in your care, let go of anything that you do not want to keep. And if all you want to keep is your memories, that's OK too.

5

You Can't Take It With You

Client: "I have a lifetime of things I've been collecting from my travels. My late husband and I traveled extensively for his work before we had children."

BBT: "How lovely. I'm sure that each of your pieces comes with a fantastic story. It will be a challenge deciding which ones to move with you to your new home now that you are downsizing, but I'm here to help."

Client: "Not challenging at all. As I said to my children, it all stays with me."

It's like the reading of a will with the deceased still alive and sitting in the room; downsizing an aging parent to smaller accomodations is an emotionally charged minefield. And not just because of the sentimental attachment to a houseful of things. There is anger, pride, greed, manipulation, relationships between parent and child or between siblings, loss of independence, and even mortality. It can all play out like the story arc of a Shakespearean drama.

Navigating the situation can be tricky but it must include **tact, maturity, transparency, and a bit of tough love.** This is not the time for miscommunications, backroom negotiations or backstabbing. Before all else, **everyone must be brought together to discuss the situation openly.** When I have mediated these kinds of gatherings, it's best that everyone places themselves in **the correct mindset—calm, kind, and compassionate, but above all, honest**. It should remain **a safe zone for all to express their individual thoughts and feelings, especially if mom or dad is fighting the inevitable move.**

* * *

I was called to help Iris downsize her family house to a one-bedroom apartment in a retirement community. Her daughters were the ones who called. They said right from the start that the two of them, along with their brother, would gladly pay my fee plus any decorating their mother wanted in her new home, with the understanding that they would not be responsible for handling any of the details, especially when it came to making decisions for or with their mother. I accepted all but the last condition of their offer. I would not single handedly take on the responsibility for the possessions in their childhood home or be left unprepared with an aging, and seemingly difficult, client. I did, however, suggest that we all sit down and I would help them and their mother get to a personal place where she could free herself of her belongings, and in turn free them of the burden. They reluctantly agreed.

I met them all at the family house, which was much grander than I anticipated. It was a huge multi-level Georgian-style mansion in Chevy Chase, Maryland. Knowing that she would be downsizing to an apartment that was roughly the size of her current foyer, I realized this was going to be a lot more difficult than I had first thought. More so once I came to learn that Iris did not want to be moved in the first place. Her children had essentially told her that she could no longer live there on her own and had sold her house against her wishes.

I'm going to be completely upfront. This situation did not end well at all. Once I tell the story of how it finally came to a conclusion, I will then proceed to tell you how I *would have* completed the work, had we gotten that far in the process. Suffice to say, a lot of planning and ordering of upholstery to decorate her new condo did take place, but ultimately everyone gave up the fight and everyone lost. (With the exception of me, who was paid my full fee, even though I was willing to take less. Her children insisted on that.)

The family and I sat down in the formal living room for tea, which had been laid out by the housekeeper.

There was Iris and her three adult children, Charlotte, Melanie, and Patrick, and Patrick's wife, Kim. Patrick and Kim were the only ones who lived nearby in Potomac; Charlotte and her family lived outside of Boston, and Melanie and her husband lived in San Francisco. Charlotte took the lead and explained that her mother was not physically well enough to live on her own even with the housekeeper coming every day. She went on to say that it wasn't fair to Kim to have to handle all the doctor appointments and errands and "demands" that came with living so close to Iris. And that the house was clearly too big for one person and it "just made sense to move forward with our plans to move Mom into an assisted living situation."

The house had just been sold. The new owners were out of the country and would not be moving in for another seven months. Iris's children arranged to rent back from the new owners to make the transition smoother for their mother. And since the condo that they had purchased for her was already vacant, we would have the luxury of a leisurely timeline to make the move. That was the last of the pros on the pro/con list.

Iris began yelling that her "self-involved children" were "trying to shut her up in a home" so they didn't have to deal with her. This led to eye-rolling and yelling back, and Kim leaving the room muttering something to me as she left, that "they were getting Iris all wound up" and that she would be "the one to deal with it all once they left." It wasn't an ideal situation by any measure.

I asked to speak with Iris alone. I could sense that there had been a lot of "talking around Mom" instead of with her and she was feeling as if control of her life had been taken away from her. It didn't help that she was a stubborn and berating woman to everyone including me. Once everyone had stepped out, I refreshed our teas and sat down opposite her so we were facing each other instead of side by side. As Iris sat in silence looking out the window attempting to ignore me, I explained to her that my job was to help facilitate a smooth transition from one home to the next and make her new home as beautiful as this one. I told her that I had already gone to the condo to take measurements and that I was extremely impressed with the way the architects had made a new modern building feel authentically traditional. I told her I was confident that she would feel at home instantly once the work was complete.

She turned to look at me with steely eyes and said, "It doesn't matter. I'm not moving."

I met her stare and said, "I don't think that's an option, but we can make the best of the situation at hand."

She huffed and narrowed her eyes and looked out the window again. "I like you, Bonnie. But I hate this."

I replied with a joke. "Then you won't feel bad about spending some of your kids' inheritance on expensive new window treatments and wallpaper, will you?" She started to laugh out loud, which brought everyone back into the room to see what was happening. That's when I took the floor for my proposal and laid out the facts.

We had less than seven months to empty the house and decorate the condo—a massive undertaking, but not impossible. I asked Iris where she would like to live in the meantime and of course she said "right here." I told her that in order to set up the condo, I would need to move her bedroom furniture there. It was my first attempt to get her to settle in at her new residence so downsizing could take place in the house without delay or interjection. She refused to let that happen, telling me I could move her bedroom furniture last, "if at all." I didn't pursue it further.

I outlined what we collectively as a group needed to discuss:

- **What items Iris wanted moved to her new home.**
- **What she wanted each of her children to have specifically.**
- **What each of her children wanted to choose for themselves.**
- **The possibility of considering an estate sale, auction, or consignment.**
- **What items she would be donating, and to what charities.**

I told her that before I left that day, she and I would walk through the main level and choose the items she wanted to take. I would then give her additional suggestions and options based on the measurements I had taken and we could make adjustments to the list from there. That's when she told me she had a favorite chair that was, without question, to be worked into the decorating at the condo.

No one could have conceived at that moment that this chair would be the undoing of everything. Melanie chimed in to say that the chair was broken and offered to buy her mother a new one, but Iris insisted she did not want a new chair, she wanted this one. I proposed a compromise. I'd send it to my furniture restorer to repair the base and replace the upholstery to suit her new decorating scheme. At the time, it seemed that everyone had found something they could agree on. But this would be the first of many painfully long, heated discussions involving nearly every piece of furniture that came into question.

For the better part of two hours I played referee while her children came and went from the room depending on their level of frustration. Even I was losing my patience with Iris. She still hadn't gotten past the fact that she was being forced to move. Nor was she at all pleased that a lifetime of acquisitions were going to her "ungrateful" kids or worse, "the junkyard." Likewise I was losing my patience with her children, who showed no compassion for the situation they had put their mother in. They wanted nothing more than to wash their hands of the situation and have me take care of all of it. Adding insult to injury, most of what Iris wanted each of them to have, they didn't want, but they were coming to blows over those things they each felt belonged to them. I admit, what happened next was not my finest hour, but I had had enough.

"OK everyone, listen up! I think I've danced around this for long enough and frankly, if you ask me to leave once I've said my piece, I will gladly go. But I think you all need to hear this. Iris, this house is too big for you. I have walked through it and there are rooms, no, I take that back, there are levels that I know you have not seen in months, if not years. You don't entertain anymore, you're struggling with the stairs, and it's draining your finances as it's falling into disrepair. Your new condo is small, I get that. It is not nearly as elegant, but it's efficient. And the community is vibrant with people and activities and all your meals are made for you. Hell, I'd move there if they took me. Did your children handle the situation wrong? Absolutely! But I am sure they were only thinking of what is best for you. And not to put too fine a point on this, but this house is no longer yours. It belongs to a new family who is letting you stay here while they are away. I know that is cruel of me to say so bluntly but it is the truth and the sooner you admit that to yourself, the sooner we can get some actual work done and move forward. I am here to make this transition happen, but I'm not going to endlessly fight about it. It's your call. What is everyone's decision?"

All were silent, as they looked back and forth between me and each other. Then Patrick spoke. "I think we can all agree we would like you to stay on this project to help us through it. Mom, do you agree?"

"I agree. With all of it. And now, I think I'm going to go lie down. That's enough for today." And with that she left the room. I thought it best to make my exit too and scheduled a time for the next day to come back when the two daughters and daughter-in-law could be there. I said I would bring fabric samples for the window treatments and the chair. And I left.

The following day, I met with Iris and her daughters and daughter-in-law. I brought with me the possible plans for how the furniture she wanted to take would be arranged and a few options of different items she owned that would fit better than what she chose. Also, based on the color schemes we discussed, I brought in upholstery fabric books for them to go through. Everything went beautifully. They chose a fabric for the chair and another for some throw pillows, and decided to repurpose the existing formal window treatments to suit the smaller windows at the condo. I sent all the instructions and measurements to the furniture restorer and his wife, a seamstress, who agreed to pick up the chair and draperies in a few days. I also contacted my mover, who was booked up for the time being so he wouldn't be able to move any pieces from the house to the condo for at least a week. This worked out just as well because two days later I received a phone call.

"Miss Bonnie, it's Lee. Your client won't let us into the house to get the chair and draperies. She says she's changed her mind."

"Jesus! OK, give me a few minutes. I'll call you back."

I texted the two daughters and daughter-in-law and waited for a reply. I didn't hear back soon enough for my patience level so I called Charlotte first. She said she had gotten my text and was already on her way to her mother's house with Kim. I told her I would meet them there.

By the time I got to the house through Beltway traffic, the upholsterer had already gone. I hoped that meant he and his assistant had gotten what they came for, but that was not the case. Inside sat Iris, in her favorite chair, in the middle of the foyer, facing the front door, ignoring Charlotte and Kim, who were pleading with her.

I walked right into the house. "OK, Iris. What's going on?"

"I've changed my mind."

"And you didn't bother to tell me? That was incredibly inconsiderate given my guys drove down here from Gaithersburg in the middle of the day."

"How much is the charge? I'll pay it."

"You're not understanding that the real problem cannot have money thrown at it. You are moving,

Iris. You have to try and find a way to see some joy in this because right now you are just choosing to be miserable."

"No! You don't understand. This is my house!"

Charlotte started to cry. I suggested Kim take her to make some tea and leave me to talk to Iris, but I asked that they please not leave in case I needed them. Once alone, I pulled a chair from the dining room up next to Iris where we sat for the next few minutes, in her foyer, facing the open front door, in silence.

"Iris, I really want to help you. Tell me how I can do that."

"I don't want to move to that place. I don't want to play bingo and eat meals with strangers. I don't like people. I want to be by myself in my house."

"I understand you completely. You and I are of like mind there."

"And this stuff is mine and I love it. You were right when you said I haven't seen most of it in years, but before we had kids, my husband and I traveled all over the world collecting these things. And you said it. There is a story behind everything I have. I had quite a life. Now my kids want me to live out my days in some old folks home. I can't think of anything more depressing."

"Have. You *have* quite a life. Look, I'm not going to pretend to know what you are going through, but I have tried to put myself in your place so I can better understand your position. Some things are already done and out of your control, so why not take control where you can? Decide to give that new place a try whether or not you join the bridge club or senior swim team. See to it that you surround yourself with your very favorite things. And make new friends on your terms. I guarantee there are people just like you there."

"That sounds nice but it's still not happening. I'm sorry, Bonnie. Please just go."

"I'm sorry too, Iris. I wish you all the best." I smiled at her and squeezed her hand. Then, leaving my notes and floor plans on the chair seat, I left.

I texted Charlotte on my way down the driveway. I told her I'd speak to her later and that I was sorry that at this point in time, there wasn't much more I could do. She texted back "I'm sorry." That was the last time I saw any of them.

* * *

About a week before the seven-month mark came to a close, I texted Charlotte, Melanie, Patrick, and Kim, offering any last-minute help at either location. Turns out, Iris refused to move to the condo so they sold it back to the facility. They were also being sued by the new owners of the house and eventually settled out of court by buying back the house at a hefty premium. Lastly, they arranged to have the housekeeper move in to take care of Iris full time so Kim would no longer have that burden. I thought to myself afterwards that that probably was the best option all along, but they unfortunately had to learn it at a substantial financial loss.

I try very hard to see all projects from the perspective of my clients. Especially when the client is not a willing participant. It's easy enough to work through a master closet for someone who has called me in to make it look pretty. By contrast, it's a battle for someone going through a life-changing event brought on as a result of circumstance instead of design. **I seek first to reassure them that I will always be respectful of their property and their wishes. I explain in detail the goals for their new residence in an attempt to get them excited for the change. I walk them through the process of how I and my associates will follow through on our schedules so they are confident I have it all under control. And then we set about doing the emotional work of letting go, by digging down to their true feelings about their belongings—** such as, is it the actual item or the story behind it, is its beauty feeding their soul, is it the practical usefulness, is it just about ownership, or perhaps, have they never given much thought to it at all? **I never discourage someone from keeping something that they truly love, appreciate, and use.** And as with advice in any other chapter in this book, downsizing our possessions does not mean stripping your things to one spoon per family member. All it comes down to is **being reasonable and honest with what you are giving purpose and space to in your home.** When you are faced with a scenario not unlike my own recently, where you are moving to a smaller home, you need to be all the more strict with yourself. The end result is being surrounded by only those things that serve you in some way and nothing that weighs you down. Literally.

Had things gone according to plan, the work schedule would have looked like this:

1. **I would have met with the family to discuss a strategy for moving into the new condo—what was going, when it would go, my decorating schedule, my contractors' schedules, and when Iris would start living there full time.**

2. **I would have discussed with Iris what pieces she wanted to give to each of her children and whomever else she wanted to gift things to. I would have also discussed with each of them arranging to have these items moved to their homes as soon as possible.**

3. **I would have discussed with the family what items they felt they wanted above and beyond what Iris was giving to each of them and mediated any disputes. Each person would get colored sticky notes. Iris would have final say. Arrangements would be made to move these pieces.**

4. I would have assembled a team, led by my
    assistant, Jesse, to help me work through
    each room sorting items of personal or
    sentimental significance, and private finan-
    cial significance, from items for donation
    and items for trash. And then dust clean all
    remaining furnishings for an estate sale.

5. I would have arranged for a dumpster to be
    delivered, to collect trash and damaged items
    from the house.

6. I would have arranged for the charity(s) of
    her choice to pick up household items, cloth-
    ing, etc.

7. I would have arranged for an estate auc-
    tioneer to host a sale and I would have been
    on hand the entire weekend to represent
    the family.

8. Once the house was free of all possessions,
    I would have scheduled a deep cleaning.
    Repairs and renovations would be left to the
    new owners unless otherwise agreed upon
    and if necessary, I would have arranged for
    those as well as a courtesy.

9. I would have had her new condo completely

decorated, staged, cleaned, and set with fresh flowers and food basics as a final gesture.

Unfortunately, I wasn't able to do any of that for them.

Nor was I able to cancel the chair fabric order before it was cut at the warehouse and even though they paid for it, Charlotte and Melanie weren't interested in keeping it. So if you ever happen to sit at my kitchen table for a meal or a cup of coffee, the fabric you'll be sitting on was originally meant for Iris's favorite chair.

6

You're Not Overwhelmed, Just Unmotivated

Client: "I know it's a disaster. I don't have any idea where to start. I should probably throw it all out."

BBT: "Great! I'll get the garbage bags!"

Client: "No! I was kidding. I just need you to help me find places to put it all."

BBT: "OK. Just so you know, the place we find may be your recycling bins."

I am a firstborn, type A, OCD-ridden home organizer. On most days I tick all the boxes on my daily to-do list. But even I fall victim to procrastination. Writing this book was a case in point. I expected it to be completely written, edited, published, and on bookstore shelves in six months. It took two years. I suppose some of that delay was my daughter's senior year of high school, selling my house, moving out of state, and negotiating the daily news cycle of a global pandemic election year... but that's not really what held up my progress. The truth of the matter was that most of what dragged out the timetable was good old-fashioned "I'll do it later." The writers' community calls it "writer's block," best described as "I'm just going to watch another five episodes of this 10-year-old sitcom and then I'll sit down to write."

As long as we're on the subject of procrastination, let me say loud and clear, it is absolutely the cause of your overwhelmedness. You are overwhelmed because the mess in front of you appears to require more energy than you can muster and therefore is too much to handle, so you decide to put it off until such a time that you seemingly will have more energy, instead of tackling even just a little bit of the larger project. "I'm overwhelmed" is just another way to say, "It's easier to throw my hands up and keep adding to the mess than to make a plan and get to work."

I understand it can be a daunting task to look at your mess, not know how to begin, and just want to close it all behind a door. To be honest, I've been in more than a few houses where I wanted to do the same thing. Believe me, I've seen some things! There was one house in particular where I jokingly suggested they just level the place. But I digress.

Let's start from the very start. Actually, it's more of a pre-start. The very first step does not require energy or manual labor or boxes being dropped off at the Salvation Army. It doesn't even require a pen and paper (though I always find any task benefits from being written down so you can see it in front of you instead of taking up headspace remembering it). **No, the absolute first step on this monumental staircase called clutter is to determine your "why." Not why you are overwhelmed. Not how you got there or what you are going to do to get out. But "why" does it matter that it's a mess? And "why" do you care to remedy it in the first place?** If you say "because I should," I will promptly thank you for your time and tell you to call me when you have a better reason.

Here's the thing. If you don't care about your mess, and no one that lives with you cares either, and no one visits you and/or you don't have anyone you'd ask anyway, and the authorities haven't been called in because there is a strange biohazard cloud above your house... then why do you want to change anything? Don't get me wrong, I personally think you would live a better life in a clean, organized, and efficient environment. What I'm getting at is if you don't really feel the need and are only considering getting your act together because you think you should, you are not going to be motivated to get it clean, much less keep it that way. **You have to personally want it and more importantly, you have to know why.**

Here's an example that may explain my point:

*If you were missing ten dollars somewhere in your overcrowded, box-laden attic, you'd probably leave it there to find one day off in the future when you were finally forced to address the clutter because you were moving or a tree fell on your roof. But if you were missing a million dollars, you'd pull every last bit of clutter out and search high and low until it was found. The point being, **if the reward is valuable enough, the job is not insurmountable. Your reward is your "why."***

No organizing project, whether it is a junk drawer or a packed-to-the-rafters garage, can move forward, much less start, without focus and commitment. That **commitment comes from understanding what exactly your end goal is. You must want to get your act together for some tangible result,** otherwise you won't be able to do the work involved to clear it out and you certainly won't be able to maintain it afterwards. Your first step before anything else is **fully understanding why this task is important to you at this time and what that ultimate achievement is that you are hoping for once the job is complete.** It is only in completely understanding your personal goals that you will have the unwavering commitment to the process that is necessary. Steer clear of vague explanations like "It's a mess so I should clean it up." Even short-term goals like "I have company coming and I've been using the guest room as a catchall so I'd better get that cleared" are not an impactful enough reply. You are looking for a forever fix, a life-changing goal. Remember that million dollars in the cluttered attic? That wasn't the best example. That was a short-term fix, too, and honestly, once you found the money you would have the means to pay someone to handle the garbage left behind. I was only using it to illustrate motivation. But your motivation does not need to be monetary, nor does it have to mean anything to anyone but you. In fact, one of the best replies to the question of why came from my client Chuck, who said, while we stood on top of the junk mail carpeting his living room floor... *"I want to be able to bring a date home."*

* * *

Chuck was in his late 30s. His apartment was on the top floor of a converted Victorian manor house in Old Town Alexandria. He had three cars sitting in the driveway when I arrived—a vintage Mercedes, a Range Rover, and a Tesla. All were buffed to gleaming perfection. I hoped for the same attention to detail upstairs. I was disappointed but not surprised. He had forewarned me, after all.

He was a semiprofessional online gamer. He used the term "semiprofessional" since his winnings were not yet his primary income but he was working towards that goal. I was curious how a nearly 40-year-old man made money playing video games, but I didn't ask. He was paying me in cash so it was honestly none of my business. As for his day job, he worked from home as a website designer ever since he'd left an IT position with a government contractor in DC. The amount of gadgets and computer equipment he owned supported that fully, as there were cords and electronics everywhere.

As Chuck walked me through the space, I was awed by the huge floor to ceiling windows (a few of which were stained glass), detailed crown molding, and the generous size of the rooms. In fact, there were three large rooms in addition to the bedroom, bath, and kitchen. It would have been a beautiful apartment were it not for the filth and chaos. Clothes and junk mail were strewn all over the floor, commingling with the dishes and takeout containers from past meals, which were sitting on top of moving boxes he was using as tables. There were by my estimate at least 60 unpacked boxes and only the bare minimum in furniture. Plus one oddly situated loveseat standing up on its end propped in a corner of the breakfast room off the kitchen.

"When did you move in?" I asked as I took some before photos to analyze later.

"About six years ago."

"So you haven't opened these boxes in six years? Is it safe to say we can pitch them?"

"After we go through them I would be willing to do that."

"Can I ask you about the loveseat on its side? No, wait! Can I guess?"

"Sure."

"You moved it in that way and never got around to putting it anywhere or even down on all fours."

"That is correct."

We both laughed.

As I inspected further, an odd pattern began to emerge. Closets and dressers were essentially bare, but the bedroom floor and the top of the dressers were piled high with clothes. The same habit appeared in the kitchen, where the cabinets were empty, but the countertops were covered with dishes and cereal boxes. Chuck, it seemed, was a visual person who needed to see his things. With that understanding, I was already devising a plan in my head for open shelving, cubbies at eye level, and removing cabinet and closet doors, but before I could create a new living space we had to declutter the old. And that would start with a conversation.

I asked him about his day-to-day life and why he hadn't unpacked in six years. His story was somewhat stereotypical of other bachelors I've worked with. He had previously worked long hours in an office with a strenuous DC commute, and once home spent most of his time growing his side businesses. He had started living in the apartment before attempting to make it his home so it never became more than a place to sleep, shower, and eat. In fact, he told me he had dated someone for two years, and in that time she had never once set foot inside. He was too worried about scaring her off with the state of his living situation. I told him that was probably a smart move.

As a result of currently working from home, however, the mess had gotten worse, and once overwhelmed with it all, he lost focus and it began to depress him. That's when he called me. He had been to a friend's house I had previously organized and was inspired to "get his life on track," a personal goal I admire greatly in my clients. When people are in that mindset, the simple act of downsizing can be profoundly life changing. It makes my job that much more fulfilling and satisfying when a client is ready for this kind of transformation.

Now aside from noticing he was not using his storage options effectively or at all, it was also obvious that he had no **lifestyle systems** in place.

NOTE: Lifestyle systems are those little procedures we all have in our homes that create efficiency. You may not even notice that they exist because they just come about naturally and give structure and sense to the flow of life. But they are ingrained in every task we do in a home from spoons resting together in a drawer to laundry detergent placed near the washing machine. Think about all the systems in your home that are just part of your routine:

→ the dish detergent on the counter next to the sink so it's readily available to use when washing dishes

→ pens and pencils in a cup on your desk for easy access when you are working, and in my case, pens already open and facing down into the pencil holder so I can pull one out and immediately write when I get an idea I want to jot down

→ a place to hang your coat, a place to put your keys, a system for backup toilet paper when you run out while you're sitting (and when you have guests coming over, make your backup supply easy to access for them; no one wants to be trapped in that situation)

When you have a second, pick a room in your home and test the theory that you are living with multiple systems in place without even knowing it. Think how much easier life would be if you learned a few more. You'd be surprised how often people make their lives more difficult by not thinking through a simple system.

For Chuck, hanging his coat on a rogue nail supporting a towel bar in the bathroom became his routine as opposed to, say, hanging his coat on a hook by the door leading out of the house.

"Do you think, once we get this place in order, if I give you a clear set of instructions on what goes where, you could get into a habit with them?" I asked.

"Absolutely. I'm a creature of habit. My habits are just terrible at the moment."

I was thrilled to hear that he was ready to make this change because it was clear that what would have been seemingly obvious to just about anyone appeared to be completely alien to Chuck. I mean, coffee cups in the medicine cabinet? He needed help.

How best do you tackle a job where you are starting with nothing but mess, with outrageous amounts of clutter, no system in place to get in back in order, indeed, not even furniture placed on all fours? The answer is simply put—**start small and build on it.** This project called for a complete overhaul and since we needed a blank canvas from the start in order to turn this place into a suitable home, step one was easy—**grab the garbage bags.**

1. **Grab a trash bag and a recycling bin and start filling it. You'd be surprised to find out that much of what is lying around as clutter is actually garbage or recycling. You can clear out a good deal of stuff with just this one step.** Now, please don't tell me, "But I haven't gone through it yet." I'll tell you the same thing I told Chuck: "That flyer for 50% off hair extensions at the Wig Barn that expired in December of 2017? I feel completely comfortable saying that it can go in the bin without consideration."

Under better circumstances, my suggestion is always to work one room at a time from start to finish starting with the smallest room in the house, which is usually the bathroom. But this was not "better circumstances." This was a full living space intervention and to be honest, my gag reflex had been kicking in for the last hour or more. We, or more appropriately I, needed to remove as much trash as possible and do so quickly. Chuck and I started at opposite ends of the apartment and worked toward the front door. I took the kitchen, breakfast room, and office, and he handled the bedroom and bathroom (which I had no intentions of dealing with without a hazmat suit) and we met in the living room. Rubber gloves are optional, but in this case they were a must. And once all the trash is bagged, it should be taken out immediately to create space.

ADVICE: Construction-grade contractor garbage bags are best for large-scale projects where you will also be throwing out a lot of heavy or awkwardly shaped items. These bags are taller and wider than the usual household trash bags, and sharp objects are not likely to puncture the reinforced plastic so there should be no leaking or dangerous edges poking through. Recycle as much as possible but know your local codes. Recycling the wrong things could lead to the whole collection being trashed at the recycling center anyway.

2. **Next, gather all items that belong elsewhere and put them back there. This is where the dirty dishes throughout your house finally find their way back to the kitchen and the discarded dirty socks on the living room floor manage to make their way into the hamper. But don't add to your mess. Wash those dishes and throw in a load of laundry. No time like the present to start cleaning.**

Since the kitchen was under my domain, I grabbed one of the empty plastic bins I bring to all jobs to use for sorting (yes, I know, but they do have their place) and asked Chuck to collect every dish, glass, and mug, including the ones in the bathroom and scattered around the apartment, then bring it all to me in the kitchen. As I loaded the dishwasher (and shhh, tossed some "filthy beyond cleaning" bowls in the trash that were no longer suitable to eat food out of), I had Chuck take another bin and collect all the errant clothes around the house and then run down to the laundry room to start the wash.

Most of you are probably not in the same state of complete chaos as Chuck was. At least I hope not. This was a much more complicated project than most. Most homes have some semblance of order, no matter how misguided, underneath the filth. Here, there was nothing to work back to. So with all the laundry either in the washer or waiting to go in and all the dishes either in the dishwasher or washed by hand, I thought it was time to take a break and discuss the bigger picture. Sometimes you need to walk away to gain a little perspective, put your thoughts in order, and charge up for the next step. Which clearly Chuck needed as I was about to explain that this was going to be a minimum of two straight weeks of work, and that I would need his input and help or he would have to give me full authority to pitch anything I felt needed to go. He said he was all in to make this change and that he had already reworked his schedule to get his assignments in after hours. His enthusiasm was infectious. I truthfully have never had a client with such a disaster on his hands and yet completely committed to the process.

We decided to grab some coffee at a nearby café. At first, I tried not to talk about the work we still had to do that day in order to prepare for tomorrow. Frankly, I was more interested in hearing more about his love life.

"So, the point of all of this change is so you can bring a date home? I need you to know that that is the best response I've ever been given. And completely valid. Your apartment is not ideal at the moment," I said with a laugh.

"Yeah. It's bad. My sister came over the other day and said it looks like the home of a drug-dealing twelve-year-old."

"I would never say that to your face, but yes. I guarantee though, when we are finished downsizing, organizing, and redecorating your place, it's going to give the same impression your cars do. Polished and put together. No one will ever suspect that it used to be a total disaster."

"Yeah, it's pretty grim. But I'm geared up. If what you say is true, I'll be dating by the weekend."

"We've barely scratched the surface, quite literally. Why don't we say, first date by the end of the month."

"Deal."

I pulled out my notebook and we started formulating a game plan. To round out the rest of the day, Chuck was going to continue to focus on **finishing the laundry, stacking flat all his clothes, and running the trash and recycling to the dump,** while my job would be to **start and complete the first round of sorting.** We also put some **thought into reassigning his space.**

3. **Before you move a thing, determine the function of each space: eating, sleeping, entertainment, reading, paperwork, hobbies, storage, etc. Then, starting in one room, begin moving things to the appropriate assigned space. This is not time for detailed work. Work with a big brush, as the saying goes. And move as much as possible to its new home. This step is about creating ease and efficiency from your clutter by giving purpose and function to the rooms in your home.**

NOTE: This is *your* home! If you want to make what is conventionally the dining area of your kitchen into your home office, go for it. Swap the living room and the family room, that's your choice. Just like assigning a spare bedroom as a craft room, this is your time to make your home make sense for how you use it. You live there! Make it your own!

My goal before I left for the evening was to do this type of sorting throughout the entire apartment. It was just going to be a first pass, just the broad strokes, but it was important that Chuck see progress that first day so he did not become disillusioned. Since it was already midafternoon I decided it was best to focus on what was out and visible and put off tackling the 60+ packed boxes for another day. They were not a priority at the moment and opening them would have only created more chaos.

4. **Don't waste your time walking from room to room searching for specific items to move to a specific space.** In other words, don't walk around the house in search of office supplies to go into the office space. **Instead, break down each room one at a time, sort and distribute the items from that one room, and move those items to their designated locations.** If it helps, grab some empty bins (I am really

shooting myself in the foot with that book title) and assign them destinations—kitchen, bathroom, office, bedroom, living room, etc. **When you are finished sorting the contents of a room into the appropriate bins, and all that is left are the things you are using in that room, carry the bin to the correct living space, empty, and move on to the next.**

Let's start in the breakfast room—you know, the one with the loveseat on its side. I knew I wanted to use that loveseat as the focal point of what would be his newly created reading nook in the large sunroom. Oh, did I not tell you that Chuck's apartment had a large corner sunroom with walls of windows spanning both sides? The light streaming in all day long was magnificent, but he was using the room as a catchall—no furniture, just boxes and piles of old magazines. He hadn't set foot inside this warm and inviting room in several years except to add to the pile. I suggested assigning it as a home office/reading area and he agreed. Truth be told, if this were my home, I would have made this room my bedroom and the bedroom into the office but I was already making so many changes to his life, I left that suggestion off the list for now. It would be easy enough to come back in a year or so and suggest a room swap in addition to some upgraded decorating; there is only so long that college castoffs can be your sole source of furnishings and no nearly 40-year-old should own a pizza-stained futon as a living room couch.

Even though that space was loaded with boxes, I managed to maneuver the loveseat through the sea of cardboard and put it down where I wanted it. Back in the breakfast room there was nothing left but a few empty trash cans, since the trash and recycling were with Chuck on their way to the dump. Making a note to remind me to create a new system to address trash and recycling, I moved the trash cans out and used this newly empty space to store all the packed cardboard boxes from around the apartment to deal with later. Continuing to push through at a steady pace, I sorted most of the apartment before Chuck got back. **Mail, random pens, computer equipment moved to what would be the home office space. Books to the reading nook. DVDs, gaming equipment to the entertainment area. Towels to the bathroom. You get the idea.** The upside to this project was that Chuck had what only seemed like a lot. With trash and recycling gone and everything moving around to more suitable locales, he didn't actually own that much. I took a quick break to make some notes of what furniture would suit his needs and tastes.

Once Chuck got back, I had him **finish the laundry and had him lay each piece flat to limit wrinkles. I told him to do the same with all the clothes still in drawers and the closet.** We would tackle clothes first thing in the morning. I also insisted he not continue working once

I'd left. He was just to pat himself on the back for getting through his first day of organizing boot camp, then rest and recharge. "Downsizing would start at dawn."

Now, I could regale you for the remainder of this chapter with the Tales of Chuck, which were frustrating in person but funny in hindsight. There was the morning when we downsized his clothes and he fought me over a pile of sentimental concert tees that he could no longer wear but insisted on keeping. It was also during that same time that I had to tell him to stop purging his pants because I was afraid he would forgo wearing bottoms entirely. We ended that day with the following conversation regarding his vast inventory of electronics:

"I didn't say I wanted to get rid of them, just put them out of the way. What are you going to do with them?"

"Drop them at a donation center. You said you don't use them."

"But I might."

"But you probably won't. Let's be honest here, you haven't set foot in this room in at least a year, more likely the six years you've lived here. If you get rid of everything you don't use, imagine the amazing space you'll have to entertain in. Besides, this old tech stuff is not your style anymore. Not a man who drives a Tesla." (Yeah, I know, that last comment was cheap and ego stroking but I had a job to do and he was putting the brakes on.)

* * *

But the stories I'd tell you would wind up being purely for entertainment value. Chuck was a special case, the specifics of which do not apply to the general public. No one needs the story details on how it took four days to go through over 50 boxes of mostly junk mail. Think about that for a second. Imagine over the course of six years, you boxed everything you would typically recycle and then lived with it, occasionally using it as furniture. That's exactly what Chuck had done. Talk about not having a system! Even handling something as trivial as junk mail seems daunting when you don't have a plan.

NOTE: Lifestyle System Hack 101: Quick Fix for Junk Mail
  → Stop it at the source by contacting those corporations and organizations and asking to be removed from their mailing lists.
  → Go paperless with the bills and statements you do want to see.
  → Go from the mailbox directly to the recycling bin and open your mail there. Junk mail, envelopes that bills came in, etc., need never enter the house.
I told you it was a quick fix.

Now for all those previously mentioned reasons specific only to Chuck, I am going to continue by breaking down the remaining steps as they apply to downsizing a typical household. So here goes. You have already:

- **collected the trash and recycling**
- **collected and washed the clothes and dishes from the entire home**
- **moved items from each room to their newly assigned spaces for that function.**

What's next? **Now you can finally start downsizing! All that work was just to get you to a place where you can finally downsize!**

5. **Grab some boxes or bags. Time to give your castoffs new life beyond your home. Donate, give to someone specific, or sell.** If you have as many old, unused items as Chuck had and are living in much the same way, I want you to seriously consider NOT considering any other option but donation. Don't burden yourself with more decisions. Choose an organization you appreciate that accepts donations, box it, drop it, and remember to ask for a receipt for your taxes. You've got a writeoff coming.

6. **Start in one room. I suggest the smallest room in the house and leveling up each time. But don't consider an entire room a single project. Break every space down into a small**

grid. At least five sections (each wall and the center) but a nine-square grid like a tic-tac-toe board is optimal for a typical room. Then, working the outside of the room in a clockwise manner from the door, work your way all the way around, leaving the center and the doorway for last. Why do it this way? First, it gives you multiple start/stop points if you need a break or need to attend to something else. Plus, at any given moment, you can see the work in one plot that you have finished and feel accomplished. Furthermore, it gives you a deliberate framework to work within so the process is not random.

7. **Access the objects in the one section you are working in. Separate and leave behind only those items that belong in that space. Remove all others to a table you have set up for sorting. Sort into donation, give, sell, or move it into the room where it belongs if you missed that on the first go around.**

Is it really that easy? It can be, but let me break it down further and in slow motion:

→ **In your mind's eye, break any space down into sections.**
→ **Determine what that section will be used for.**

→ **Remove anything that does not meet that new function.**

→ **Place the items you removed on a separate table and sort into at least two piles: purge and keep.**

→ **Move onto the next section in the room. Do not concern yourself with organizing, decorating, or cleaning any section at this point. We are focusing on downsizing.**

But downsizing is what you're not sure about. How do you decide what stays and what goes? Well, all the chapters in this book give you the practical and basic advice on the how to's of downsizing your stuff, but let's have some fun with this. Here are a **few of my quick and quirky rules for pitching any room:**

→ **Bathroom:** If it's not part of your routine be it daily, weekly, or monthly, pitch it. If it's been opened, it goes in the trash. Unopened, donate. We all have made the mistake of an impulse purchase of a shampoo that claims to give our hair volume and bounce, used it once and nearly thrown up from the scent on our heads all day. You don't have to bear the burden of that mistake forever. Get rid of it.

→ **Bedroom:** Chapter 1 breaks down downsizing your clothes, but what else are you housing in your bedroom that does not belong there? I know there are some of you out there that use your bedroom to hide things when you have company coming. Your bedroom should be an oasis, a place of peace and serenity where once you wake up, you are recharged and rejuvenated by the beautiful environment surrounding you. Tripping over a laundry basket filled with the kids' toys that you gathered before the neighbors stopped over is not likely something that will feed your soul for the day ahead. If it doesn't provide relaxation, it doesn't belong in the bedroom. Move it out.

→ **Kitchen:** Are you keeping the containers from every food product and takeout order to use as plasticware? Have you now amassed enough to serve hundreds of hungry people your leftovers? Be reasonable. You don't need every last one. Least of all the ones that have tomato sauce stains and microwave melt. Recycle them.

→ **Office:** Get a shredder. Period. If you ever need an old copy of your Home Depot credit card statement from January 2003, Home Depot will have it. Honestly, beyond your taxes or legal documents, shred it all! Bills are all available at the source and online. So are taxes or legal documents for that matter, but hold onto those just in case.

→ **Dining room:** A football-shaped platter, a cracked crystal punch bowl, and leftover paper Easter bunny napkins sit on a dining room table. No, that's not the start of a "three men walk into a bar" joke. If you've got leftover napkins from past holidays, use them up for everyday dinner. If you haven't hosted a football gameday party in years because your neighbor has the big screen TV, consider passing that platter onto the next host with a pile of nachos. And seriously, a cracked punch bowl is garbage whether it's from Target or Tiffany's. Throw it out!

→ **Family room:** Your kids are in high school but you still have VHS tapes of Clifford and The Wiggles. I bet you don't even have a VHS player anymore, or at least not one that works. Those should immediately go in the donation box. Same with the DVDs if you've been streaming those same movies anyway. Hold them back for a yard sale if you'd like but I'm going to be honest here, you aren't going to get more than 50 cents to a dollar for any of them.

→ **Living room:** Your formal for-company-only room is always neat as a pin. In fact, you only ever venture in there to dust. Take another look and attempt to edit ten percent if not more of your tchotchkes. Clear surfaces are far easier to keep clean than ones with "puts" (my grandmother's word for things you put around a room) everywhere.

→ **Playroom:** I know this one is tough. We all want our children to have the best of everything and the best start in life. But kids have their favorites and that's enough. More importantly, it has been proven that all the bells and whistles don't do nearly as much for a child's development as simple creative play, which can come from anything—think of the old "loved the box it came in more than the toy" scenario. So weed your children's toy collection down to a select few. Hold some back to rotate in when they tire of what they have. But a good rule of thumb is not to go overboard, because it's just sensory overload. Save unopened toys to regift or return. Share the wealth with Toys for Tots during the holidays. Sell them online and put the money in a college fund. I promise your children will have wonderful, lively childhoods without every Little People set available from the toy store (true story). From my own experience, my daughter was happiest with a sheet of stickers that came in the promotional mail from a wildlife rescue charity, and she managed to get into some very prestigious colleges. My point is, less is more when it comes to toys. Purge accordingly.

Now these are not all the tips and tricks, just some of the fun ones. The point here and at every stage of this book is to be reasonable with what you need and what you want. I'm not here to suggest you give it all away and live with just what you can carry. What I'm attempting to point out is that you have more than you know you have, which means it serves no purpose for you. Get rid of it. Let's move on.

8. **Tell yourself you're going to complete one section and if you are feeling up to more, move on. But always take a microbreak to appreciate your finished area. And never start any block you can't finish.** The reason being, completing one task at a time will give you a feeling of accomplishment. This will motivate you to keep going. It will also give you a clear starting point if you stop and come back.

Chuck and I were on a roll after our morning argument over clothes. By the end of the workday we had completely downsized the entire apartment. Now remember, he didn't have much and we still hadn't opened the boxes to discover what all was inside, but small victories are just as empowering. We loaded all the donations into my vehicle and with an hour until the charity drop location closed, I bid him goodnight. I told him to enjoy his new space from which he could see the sunset and I would see him in the morning for round two.

9. **Just like breaking down a large room into smaller areas, so too should you continually sort items as you go, into smaller and smaller assortments until you have what stays and what goes. Even areas you have already gone through can benefit from a second pass.**

This is fine tuning at its best. And once you experience how clear spaces and clearly defined areas make you feel, you'll want to keep going. A great example of this is a hotel room. Clean, efficient, everything you need, not overdone decoratively and yet not austere, certainly no clutter except what you bring with you, everything in its place. How do you feel when you open the door? Don't you immediately feel your body exhale in peace? Don't you flop down on the bed and say to yourself, ahhhh? Don't you want to live like that in your own home every day? You certainly can, and it's achieved simply with less.

I started this chapter by bringing up the subject of procrastination. Ultimately, being overwhelmed is a perfect excuse not to start at all. It's a roadblock of your own making. And the longer it takes you to jump in, the bigger the problem gets, which only makes the whole situation more overwhelming. We all go through it, but don't let it move in and take over your home. **Determine your "why," use it to motivate you, jump into the task in front of you, and when you have completed the job at hand, you will no longer be overwhelmed with your clutter.** Simple enough.

Working with Chuck took the full two weeks. In a fantastic twist, while we were downsizing and donating, a local artist was requesting old computer pieces, cables, and aux cords for a sculpture project he was working on and he even picked them up; the universe is an amazing place! After clearing out so much, I gifted Chuck with professional cleaning services before I put lifestyle systems in place—think hooks everywhere. And lastly, we had a blast furniture shopping; he had more style than I had given him credit for.

I have to admit I had my doubts that Chuck could keep it the way it was when I left, so I called him a month later to see how he was doing. He laughed and said he was making dinner for his new girlfriend. I did tell you; it changes lives.

7

Yard Sale Bargains Can Lead to Bankruptcy

Client: "I love yard sales, estate sales, flea markets. I buy things, then sell them on eBay. I always make a profit. Sometimes twenty times more than I paid for them. It's a growing business."

BBT: (looking into an open closet spilling into the room) *"So these items here, are they ones you haven't listed yet?"*

Client: "No, those are ones that didn't sell."

I have always had a not-so-secret dream of owning my own home design store. A mix of new and old, traditional and modern, a carefully curated collection of nonessential sensible splurges of home decor and art, garden accessories, and children's creative learning items. You could say that the business of retail is a passion of mine. I love it all! From choosing and buying the inventory, to merchandising the showroom vignettes, to providing top-notch customer service. And when it comes to the secondhand resale market, the appeal of searching for that unpolished gem, shining it up, and selling it to the highest bidder is one I completely understand. But unfortunately, the rate of failure is astounding! All too often people enter the world of retail based on the idea that "it would be fun to own a store" and yes, it would be, if all you had to do was create window displays and take beautifully staged marketing photos. But it's so much more than that—at least 50% of the time, it's a money losing proposition.

*   *   *

Even the most successful resale sellers have a lengthy list of regret purchases but somehow that was not the case for my client Michelle, whose mantra was "Clutter and Debt with No Regret." As she put it, "It's like gambling; sometimes you win, sometimes you lose, but you always have fun." Fun, that is, until your sister has to pay your mortgage.

It was Michelle's sister Monica who called me. I told her that I would be happy to meet with the two of them but that unless Michelle herself was onboard with this, I would not be taking on the project. Monica understood my terms and we set up a meeting.

Holy moly! Imagine one of those reality shows like "Hoarders" but with the clutter all sorted by category in clean, neatly stacked boxes, about waist high in every direction, with just a pathway to get from room to room. Across the entirety of the main floor of Michelle's house, there was no visible furniture other than a folding chair in front of an end table that served as her desk. In all honesty, it was organized beautifully so I had to give her some credit.

Each room, I was told, had a theme even though nothing was labeled. For that, Michelle just knew. "I know exactly what I have. I don't have to write it down. It's all in here," she said, pointing to her temple. "I try to buy in the original box with original tags because I know those are worth more but I don't worry about it too much because I pick things up cheap. Estate sales are great for that. Collectors die and their families just want to get rid of it. By the time I show up, they're practically paying me to take it away. They don't know what it's worth but I do. I look the value up in this app I bought for my phone as I find things. Then I turn around and sell it, sometimes for ten, twelve times what I paid for it. I have never sold anything for less than double what I paid."

"That is amazing. Where do you sell?"

"A couple different places. My neighbor owns an antique store where I have a corner set up. I pay her $50 a month for the space. I usually make it back. eBay is where I make the most money and have the most fun. You'd be surprised at the things I have sold and sent all over the world. I just sent an African-American Barbie to Hungary."

"That *is* fun! Sounds like you've got a good system in place. So ladies," I said, looking from one to the other, "how exactly can I help you?"

Michelle turned to Monica and said, "I don't know why my sister asked you here."

"I asked Bonnie here because I've had to pay your mortgage the last three months because you're broke from buying crap!"

Wow! No punches pulled between these two. I would have excused myself but it was like watching a trainwreck that you can't take your eyes off of. They screamed at each other for a good 20 minutes wherein they covered everything from ripped favorite childhood sweatshirts to Monica not helping with Michelle's late husband's funeral plans. As they exhausted themselves, I stepped in.

"OK, ladies. Let me tell you what I see here. Monica, you want your sister to take better care of her finances so she can support herself, pay you back, and not borrow again. And you, Michelle, want your sister to trust you to handle your own money but you need more time to get your business up and running before you can pay her back. And maybe you also want her to stop judging your choices since grieving can be difficult. Do I have that right?"

Monica spoke first. "She and her husband couldn't

stand each other. If she's grieving it's because he left most of his money to the kids that don't speak to her."

"Please, this is way too much information for me. I'm going to have to cut you both off right here. You're not ready for this process," I said, gathering my bags.

At this point, Michelle was in tears. "I'm going to pay her back, I'm just not there yet. And I want her to stop hovering over me, telling me this isn't a business when I'm trying to make it one."

"I don't see you working to make that happen," Monica said, voice cracking. "You are constantly spending on garbage. Jesus, don't you have enough already? Look at this place!"

I could see that this was not going to be an easy assignment for me and I had to take back some control of the situation. Given the fight they so freely had in front of me, I felt comfortable to be a little brutal.

"Alright, there are only 20 more minutes left of my free hour consultation. Here is what we are going to do. Michelle, your sister cannot continue to pay your mortgage. I'm not sure how you planned to pay her back and get a handle on your own finances without a steady income. A paying part-time job might help. I know what it feels like to want something for yourself and just need more time to prove it, so I have an idea for you that I'll get to in a second. Monica, I'll tell you what was once said to me with regards to giving money to family—'give what you feel comfortable not getting back.' You kinda knew what you were getting yourself into. That's not to say Michelle is off the hook from paying you back. But if I do my job right, you'll get your money back and Michelle won't have to borrow from you again. Now, here is my proposal."

I proceeded to outline a plan that would give Michelle the best chance of paying her sister back in a timely fashion while also getting herself set up with a small but steadier income stream. And to reduce the extra burden of my fee, I agreed to take a cut of the proceeds off the top of anything made in the first three months instead. It was certainly a risk, but truth be told I was excited to stretch my retail muscle again.

First things first, these two had to hug it out. We were all in this together. And on that high note, I excused myself saying I'd be back in the morning ready to get to work. In the meantime, I asked Michelle to **pull out what paperwork and receipts she had, as well as text me the username and password of her eBay account, the address of her friend's antique store, and a list of all the local dealers in a 20-mile radius**. I was jumping in with both feet. I was invested in this and had no intention of losing money on this deal. Michelle was treating this as a hobby when what she needed to do was to treat it like the serious business she pretended it was. To show her what needed to be done, I needed her to give me the reins for the next few weeks. It was going to be fast paced and a bit frenzied but I wanted her to see that with focus and some direction she could make this part-time hobby into a full-time career.

ADVICE: If you are in the habit of buying up collections of items in hopes of netting some profits by reselling, know a little something about what you are buying and take an active interest, if you don't already have one. If you can't stand old transistors and CB radio parts, it doesn't make much sense to try to be in the resale market for them, even if the market is hot for such things. Buying and selling is a tremendous use of time and money. Enjoy every phase of the process; it makes all the difference in how you present your merchandise. Reselling items you actually love is much easier than reselling ones you couldn't care less about.

The plan I was about to implement for Michelle and Monica is the same I'd give to any client looking to cash out on the clutter they have collected, except in this case, it was a full-scale attack on her debt as well, so **I wrote up some "commandments":**

- → No further purchases until Monica is paid in full.
- → No further purchases until monthly expenses are being paid on time.
- → No further purchases until inventory is cut by 30%.
- → This is your full-time focus until this business is successful enough for it to work for you.
- → SELL! SELL! SELL! In any way possible, to anyone willing!

After reading the plan to them the next morning, we all signed at the bottom and taped it to the wall above the computer. Now to get to work! Michelle, Monica, and I sat down for a quick meeting. **I outlined what was going to be happening in the next few days**.

1. **WALKTHROUGH AND NOTETAKING:** Michelle was going to walk us through all the rooms where inventory was housed, **explain her organizing process and show how each room was sorted**, during which Monica would take notes. Unfortunately, Michelle had no records of what she paid when she purchased the items so she had no way of knowing if profits were being made. (A huge no-no if you are calling yourself a business.) What we did have in our favor at this moment was that **selling the inventory at any reasonable cost was the only goal.** She needed to **liquidate for cash.** Even if that meant at a loss. Of course, with no records, we would have no way of knowing.

2. **SOCIAL MEDIA:** Monica's daughter Erin would be joining us at my request. I enlisted her to handle the **social media marketing and sales**. To this point, Michelle used **eBay** exclusively but was not taking advantage of **free sales platforms like Facebook Marketplace**

or local Google Groups. She didn't even have **Facebook or Instagram pages for advertising and marketing purposes**. Erin would be in charge of that, as well as **photographing for daily online posts and the upcoming event** I had planned.

3. **SALES EVENTS:** Which led me to the event I planned for the next day. I had called every name on the list that Michelle had given me plus a few others. With the benefit of Michelle's organizing skills, I took advantage of the sisters' motivation to get this event scheduled as soon as possible. **All the area antique dealers, second market collectors, and people I thought might be interested were invited to come to her home for a private sale.** The goal? **Reduce her overall inventory and net enough to pay** Monica back at least in part.

4. **eBAY BRANDING:** Michelle's online presence was not branded to bring in any big buyers. It was merely a personal account where she posted items at her leisure. My goal was to **brand it like an online store with scheduled events and days where buyers could count on new inventory.** There would also be a **restructuring of how buyers could pay plus incentives like free shipping on larger orders.**

5. **IN-STORE PROMOTIONS:** Michelle did not pay much attention to the **booth she had within her friend's antique store.** She set it up and left it up to fate. There was much more that could be done in the way of **merchandising, signage to promote her online businesses, plus advertising to serious local dealers about future "dealer days."**

Michelle's head was already swimming. It was a mix of excitement and loss of control. I explained that I wasn't trying to take any of this away from her. I was teaching her how to handle it for when she was on her own as a sole proprietor but first I would be with her every step of the way as she got set up.

With the meeting wrapped up the three of us got into the thick of things, opening boxes and assessing just what we were working with. She did have a system but I explained that reworking it a bit would be better for the dealer sale. Rolling up our sleeves, we moved the bins around—dolls/toys/figurines in one room, china/crystal/silver in another, handbags/shoes in the last. Thankfully that was the bulk of it. Things that did not fit in those categories I suggested we deal with another day, hoping to perhaps convince her that they **would be best donated to take advantage of any tax writeoff. We separated each room into sections, divided the inventory, and hung signs on the walls so buyers would be able to go to the area best**

suited to their expertise. As for pricing, Michelle had the **latest appraisal app** but I warned her that there likely would be **lots of negotiating.** I promised to be with her and we would take it slow and work out a fair price but to **keep in mind that the focus was to earn as much as possible while reducing her overall inventory.**

With that organized, we completed a few more items like **calling in some family and friends to be stationed in each room to keep an eye on things during the sale, setting up the "cash wrap" area, and staging the space with new, bright-white light bulbs**. I was really happy with the way it all turned out. By this time, Erin had shown up and had gotten right to work **photographing the spaces, putting out the photos in a reminder email to the dealers for the next day, and posting on social media.** She also took it upon herself to **set up a white box to photograph each item for online sale.** I knew immediately she was going to have to be given a bigger cut than originally promised since she so clearly was going to be amazing in this role. While she worked on that the three of us took a quick trip to the antique shop to check out Michelle's booth.

The store as a whole was in need of a makeover. There were a few customers looking around but I didn't notice anyone buying. Like many other antique stores, this one was in an old farmhouse. Michelle's booth was in the first room right off the front door and took up nearly the entire far corner of the room; an ideal spot if you have a chance to choose your location. The problem was that the room was poorly lit and crowded with junk from other dealers, plus had a musty smell of mildew—I'm sure most customers scanned the room from the doorway without stepping in and then moved on to other parts of the house. **How could Michelle remedy this? Bringing in a lamp for one. Scented candles (even unlit) for another. Moisture catchers. Seasonal single-colored tablecloths for cohesiveness. And most importantly, giving her booth a story, perhaps all Barbies for the month, then all china place settings the next. Signage with her social media info and events calendar was my final suggestion.** We made up a list and left. We'd tackle this after the dealer sale. For now it was back to the house to work on cleaning up her eBay site.

NOTE: Most of you will never have to put this kind of large-scale system in place for your collection of castoffs, but if you are really packed in with stuff to sell, know that there is always someone out there willing to buy it for a certain price. You just have to know your market and give them a shopping experience. You know what I mean by a shopping experience, right? It's the same reason you bought it: The bargain. The pretty packaging. The atmosphere of the store. The customer service. It's all part of the allure of the shopping experience.

On the day of the private dealer sale, everyone was in good spirits. We had a line of nearly 10 customers before we even opened the doors. Erin's nine-year-old daughter acted as **greeter, telling everyone who entered what things were in what room.** Erin was handling the cash wrap area and I instructed her to **get detailed information from each customer so we could contact them about future events, as well as any possible inventory that met their interests.** During the sale we were getting requests for items not in the assortment available, but I was certain Michelle had something appropriate in the castoffs out back. **Not wanting to lose a customer, we opened the backyard to shopping as well.** Turned out that what I suggested be donated as random one-offs wound up being as big a seller as the items organized inside. Even I learned that nothing is off limits when you have people eager to buy.

When the day was done and the last of the dealers had gone, we closed up and ordered pizza for all the hungry volunteers. Michelle and Monica certainly had a strong support system of family and friends who not only **kept their areas neat, but sold merchandise like experienced salespeople, even helping to carry things to cars.** After that, we all sat down with Erin to await the final total. Having sold by my estimate somewhere between 15–20% of her inventory—which far exceeded my expectations—the total came to just over $3100.00. For a last-minute, first-time, pulled-together sale, that was not too shabby. In fact, it was exceptional! Michelle paid me and Erin our cuts, and gave the rest to Monica who, in a tender moment of sisterly love, gave it back to her and told Michelle to hold onto it so she could feel good about the changes she was making to her life. What a day!

Next day, armed with a floor lamp, scented oils, and new matching tablecloths, Michelle and I dismantled her booth at her friend's antique shop before store hours. Michelle took my previous suggestion and **decided to dedicate the month to a specific theme**—figurines. First step, **remove all items not in that category, box, and store** under the table (no need to lug it all home when she could use it the following month). Erin had **created a new logo and had a banner rush ordered** (Erin was really good at this!), which we promptly hung above the section of the room that Michelle called her own. Then, after setting up the lamp and tablecloths, we unboxed the figurines she had packed after the private sale. Michelle arranged them according to her own methods. I did not interfere. This was her domain. My job was to make sure all her information was posted clearly and prominently without the signage being obtrusive. **Her eBay, Facebook, and Instagram accounts were all listed, as was a list of her specialties (Barbies, Hummels, etc.) and an instruction to call for any requests.** The beauty of this situation was it really was a "set it and forget it" scenario. She didn't have to work hard and it **gave her**

a regular, albeit small, income stream to add to the others. With all that in place, we locked up and headed back to the house.

Next, we discussed the agenda going forward:

1. **Put all the dealer information into the computer and send them each a thank-you email for attending the sale. Include links to eBay, Facebook, and Instagram, as well as the antique store booth. Also, expand the original search of dealers to 50 miles and send them any info as well as upcoming event information.**

2. **Create a calendar, listing the theme each month for the antique store as well as days and times to set it up.**

3. **Create a monthly email to send to dealers and collectors to promote the sale in the antique store, as well as plan quarterly private dealer sales at the house.**

4. Erin was to **continue to update Facebook and Instagram daily with photos she would take at her discretion**. Erin had already created social media pages on both that were business specific using the new logo she had created. I asked that she also **do a deep dive on those**

platforms to "like" any other businesses in
the same secondhand, antique, vintage, or
collectibles categories and perhaps consider
a collaboration or cross promotion.

5. Erin was also to begin **utilizing Facebook
Marketplace to see how sales compared to
eBay in an attempt to make the move off the
fee-based site.**

6. Lastly for Erin, she was to continue **to photograph the inventory with the white box
for use on eBay and continue to service all
online sales. She had already stripped the
page, added the new logo, and begun posting
each item over again for a consistent look.**
She astounded me. I asked her why she never
considered doing this type of business on
her own and she explained that the dynamic
between her mother and aunt had soured her
on the idea most of her adult life. That made
complete sense to me.

With our discussion complete, Michelle and I
started the last piece of the puzzle—reorganizing the
inventory she had left. Keeping her original system in
place, all I asked that she do was **consolidate what was
left to free up some bins and in the process consider
selling some off in a "dollar deal" sale at the antique**

store or donating them directly. These would be items that were not in ideal condition or did not fit a category she was now focusing on. We spent the rest of the afternoon doing just that. In the end, she asked me if I would mind dropping the castoffs at Goodwill on my way home. She said she could use the writeoff. Of course, I did not mind at all.

* * *

So this wasn't a typical chapter about downsizing. **This chapter is less about choosing what goes than it is about how to get rid of it**. Remember that in your home this is about getting rid of stuff, not making room to bring in a rotating supply like Michelle, but the principles still apply. **Let's break it down if you are going to sell either online or at a yard sale:**

1. **Group items together.** Whether it's all children's clothes or vinyl LPs, it's important to specialize so it appears not to be a hodgepodge of junk but a collection of important pieces.

2. **Go to the source.** Find dealers or collectors who specialize in those items you have and try to negotiate a sale for the whole lot.

3. **Post on social media.** It's free advertising as well as a built-in audience base.

4. **"Package" your product.** When selling online, try to make it look like a store where you put in a little effort if you are attempting to make this into a business. The effort will either result in a better price or a quicker sale or both.

5. **Cross promote with other businesses, create events to lure the best clients, offer incentives for buying multiples, and/or give a portion to a charity as a benefit of the sale.** All quick and easy ways to boost profits. Just takes a bit of creativity and legwork.

I'd like to say that three months later Michelle had paid Monica back all the money she owed her and paid Erin in full for all her time. That was not the case. But she was that much closer. She did pay me my percentage off the top and repaid one mortgage payment that she had borrowed from Monica. Most importantly, in that time, she hadn't purchased any additional inventory nor did she borrow more money. She still had roughly 70–75% of her original inventory to work with, and a solid plan in place for all her sales outlets. She had made excellent connections with quite a number of dealers during her sale at home and even received two calls from referrals looking for specific handbags. And the next dealer sale was being advertised to a larger market. As for Erin, she loved working with her aunt so much that she asked her if she could become a full partner in building the business; ideal for her since she was a stay-at-home mom. It was a win all around. All that, and I got to "play store" for a while.

Before leaving, I sat down to talk to Michelle about what and how to buy for the future. Things like **only buying what interests you, only buying within your budget, and only buying when you are in desperate need of new inventory.** Then she said the words I was hoping she would say from the start: "I never thought there'd be anything better than that rush from buying, but oh my god, selling feels even better!"

My work here is done.

8

Don't Hide Your Joy in a Box

BBT: "What's in these boxes here?"

Client: "Those are collections for my children. I started them when each child was born to commemorate birthdays, achievements, special events. I'm going to be doing the same for my grandbaby on the way."

BBT: "What a nice idea. I can work them into the decorating plans if you'd like."

Client: "No. They have to stay in the boxes to keep them nice."

I collect pottery. I don't collect a certain artist's work or a specific technique. I collect what I fall in love with. Every individual piece makes me grin happily, from the hand-thrown pot I watched being made on a trip to

149

Santa Fe, to the bud vases I found discarded in the book section at the thrift store. The fact that en masse they all coordinate is simply a product of my tastes. I'm drawn to all things blue and green, and I have a soft spot for pieces that have what others might consider flaws. In fact, the more flaws they have, the more I like them. Each one is special for its appearance as well as how I came to own it. All together they make me absolutely giddy. They sit as a collection on a long buffet table directly across from my desk and when I look up from my laptop and see them, they feed my soul. Suffice to say, I appreciate and understand the joy of collecting.

The rush of stumbling upon your prize in a dusty antique store or having the winning bid at auction or being one of the first 50 customers in line on the day it is released; these are all part of the joy of collecting. But the fun is not just in the acquisition. For me the fun snowballs. From cleaning it up to finding its place of honor among the others, the true value is in seeing it and cherishing it and appreciating it as often as possible. So I think you can guess what my feelings are when a client speaks proudly about spending any kind of money on things intended for someone else but that are instead stored with them in the original box out of sight to keep them nice. Whew! If you haven't guessed, I have strong negative opinions about that scenario.

* * *

Tara had called me in not for an organizing project but for a decorating project. Her first grandbaby was on the way and she wanted to convert her spare room into a nursery since she would be taking care of the baby on weekdays while her son and daughter-in-law were at work. The room was currently being used as storage for three separate collections of figurines she had bought for each of her three children over the years. Each individually boxed item had the name of its recipient, the date it was gifted, and for what occasion it was given written on a sticky note adhered to the box, and all the individual boxes were stored in larger plastic tubs with the single name of the future owner. Very neat and also very unnecessary. Because each figurine was dated, writing the date was unnecessary as was writing the occasion since the figurines themselves represented that. It would have been enough to put them in the appropriately labeled box for each child. But wait? Weren't these all gifts? Why then were these things here?

"So Tara, what is your plan for these boxes?"

"Well, I can't store them in the basement or garage since they say you have to keep them in mint condition to keep their value and I worry they will get musty. I thought you could find a way to store them in the closet or under furniture and hide it with a dust ruffle or something."

"We could do that. But if I'm being honest, this is a substantial collection. Don't you want to enjoy it? I

Stop Buying Bins

could work them into the decor of the room. Or maybe your children take what's theirs?"

"Oh, they all say it's best if I keep them, you know, since they have always been here and kept temperature controlled and the boxes might get dented moving them. No, I really think I want to just keep them here."

Your adult children all say it's best if you keep them? That's code for they don't want them. Temperature controlled? They are figurines, not furs. Boxes might get dented? Are these collections you plan to sell or ones that were supposed to be gifts over the last 30-plus years that you never actually gave them? Not wanting to dig too much further with this line of questioning, I said "OK, so tell me what you are looking to do in this nursery—style, color, budget. What do you imagine for the space?"

"Well, we don't know if it's a boy or a girl, so maybe just white. I was thinking of something Pottery Barn–looking because I know that's what my daughter-in-law likes. And for budget, I could spend about $500." She said that last part in such a way that it was clear she felt that was more than enough.

NOTE: Before you hire a decorator, be mindful of what goes into their job. It is not just offering you their opinion on color samples and furniture placement, which in and of itself is worth some kind of financial compensation. You are paying for their knowledge and expertise and their ability to understand your vision and see it through to completion. They are sourcing the items, which may include bargain hunting or negotiating deals with vendors. They are vetting servicepeople and amassing a team of professionals to carry out the work you need handled, from painting to carpentry to moving. They are coordinating schedules of all work to be done within the homeowners' time parameters as well as being on site to oversee the work. It is work that can be done with a tight budget in mind but it is never going to be cheap. If you have "up to $500" to spend on an entire space, especially one without any furniture, your best option is to do the work yourself. Even then, you will likely go over budget.

"OK. Do you have any of the pieces for the room already? Crib, changing table, rocking chair, that sort of thing? I'd like to measure them."

"No. I thought that's something you do."

"It can be. But with your budget, the crib alone will be at least a few hundred. Painters the same. And there's the other pieces of furniture, plus a rug, window treatments. And then there is my fee."

"Oh, so how much will the whole thing cost?"

"I can work up plans today and get you an answer tomorrow. The fee for my detailed plans and shopping lists will be $75.00 but that will come off the cost of the overall fee if you hire me for the project. If you don't go with me, you'll have everything you need to make doing it on your own very easy."

"I had no idea that decorating cost so much."

"It's not so much the decorating as it is calling in a decorator," I said with a laugh. "But I'd like to offer a suggestion. It would be best if your children took what boxes are theirs in order to make room for this new little one on the way. I imagine there will be other grandbabies in the future to use this room, so all your children will benefit from what you do now. Just a thought. Why don't you talk it over with your children?" I thought about adding "Or, maybe if they agreed to have you sell the collections off, you could put the earnings towards decorating the room," but I didn't think she would be receptive to that.

"No, I'll be keeping them here. None of them need extra stuff at their houses. It's fine here."

"OK then. I'll get you the notes by tomorrow. Thank you, Tara. It was a pleasure meeting you." I left suspecting that she would likely not book my services, but seeing as she had already sent me an electronic payment for $75 before I got back in the car, I headed home to work on her proposal.

On the drive, I mulled over what she had initially said to me about her children wanting *her* to hold onto the lifetime of collectibles she gifted to them. They were never really gifts. These figurines were gifts she bought for herself to remind her of milestones in the lives of her children, purchased under the guise of gifts for them. If she wasn't going to let them go, I had to convince her that it was a missed opportunity to not display them.

ADVICE: When it comes to anything that takes up space in your home that is not useful or brings you no joy to see it, please be very honest with yourself. What possible value, emotional or financial, could there be in spending any amount of money on things you hide away? Why take up the square footage in your home? What is the reasoning behind buying gifts for someone else only to store them in your own home for "safe keeping"? More so, why keep them in mint condition, pristine in original packaging, if you have no intention of selling them? Especially when you need the money? The answer is none. If you love them, put them out so you can see them. If you are storing them to maintain their value, sell them when you need the money. If they belong to someone else, give them to them. Please.

I sent off the decorating plans by email the next day. I also sent an additional "bonus" project for a glass front wall-mounted curio cabinet large enough to hold many if not all the figurines. My idea was to show Tara that by having them out, she could talk to her new grandbaby about all the milestones in the lives of his/ her father and aunt and uncle. My first choice would be for her to consign them for sale, but this idea might at least get them out of boxes.

Estimate for Nursery Project:
- Painting of the walls, trim, interior closet, and doors by a painter.
- Sourcing the crib, changing table, rocker and ottoman, rug, and window treatments, all from IKEA. (Bedding purchased by the client.)
- Assembling of flat pack furniture by a handyman.
- Consultation, design, and project management fee.
  Total: $1875.00
  Cost of furniture alone: $750.00

This was truly a stripped-down price. It was clear that $500 was not going to be enough as that didn't even cover the cost of IKEA furniture. She discussed it with her son, who offered to split the cost with her, and work got underway. As for the lifetime of boxed collectibles collecting dust? I brought that part up with Tara while she was admiring the work the painters were doing.

"So Tara, there's still time to get a curio in here. The piece I found is on hold at the vintage market in town. I can have it sent over, my handyman can hang it, and the painters can paint it to blend right in with the wall. Then I can fill it with all those pretties you have stacked there," I said, pointing to the boxes now in the corner of her living room. "Let me add that I am so committed to this looking beautiful, that I've already spoken with the dealer and gotten them down to $175 from $350. And

I'll even waive my fee. You'd just pay for the handyman's labor. What do you say?"

"Ummm. Do you really think it will go?"

"Painted? Without a doubt!"

"OK. Yes, let's do it." I put my arm around her shoulder and squeezed in for a side hug, then pulled out my phone and started making calls.

When I left for the day, the curio had already been delivered and fitted to the wall with extra supports so there was no way it was going to come down (plus, it was high enough off the floor that no child could reach it to pull on it anyway). The plan for tomorrow was to have the curio painted and the furniture assembled. I planned to use the time while I was there supervising work to start unboxing Tara's collections. They were pretty, I had to give her that, but until this moment, no one was enjoying them in the slightest.

Three days later, I asked Tara to step into her grandbaby's new nursery for the first time. Upon seeing it all set in dreamy whites and sand colors, she was speechless, then she started to cry. It was "her" collections that touched her the most. I explained that even though there were three shelves and I could have displayed each child's collection on a shelf of their own, I chose instead to group them like a timeline. I showed her that the last bit of space was for the newest addition to her family.

"You were right, Bonnie. You were so right. I should have had these out all along."

"Well, now you can share your stories with your grandbaby so it all worked out in the end. I'm so glad you like how it turned out. These are meant to be enjoyed."

* * *

MY ADVICE ON COLLECTIBLES

→ **Collect what you love.** Don't collect anything just because you think it will be more valuable with time. Don't collect for other people until you know they collect that sort of thing. Collect for you, what you love, on your terms, and only for you!

→ **Display it.** "If you've got it, flaunt it." "Don't hide your light under a bushel." "Use it or lose it." No point in owning a closetful of boxes. Enjoy it by seeing it. (NOTE: Once you display everything, no need to hang onto the empty boxes unless your lifestyle is one where you move every two years like military personnel. Otherwise, just recycle them.)

→ **Mint condition is for dealers only.** If you have no intention of selling anything, mint condition is not a consideration. Don't add that burden to the mix.

→ **Don't be guilted into needing every piece of a collection.** Again, buy what you love. If #4 of 20 doesn't appeal to you, don't buy it. Complete collections are only important if you are going to sell them and even then, if someone else really wants what you have, they won't care.

→ **Don't collect for others.** Unless you are adding to a collection of their own creation, it's essentially a nongift. Giving someone something that they don't want or like, some with a significant price tag, forces them to keep it under some sense of faux importance. Knowing if they collect and what they collect is a completely different story. (See a collecting story of my own below.)

→ **DON'T KEEP ANYTHING YOU DON'T WANT!** Was it collected for you and you don't collect that sort of thing? Get rid of it. Do you collect something but you're not crazy about what someone else added to your collection? Get rid of it. Have you grown tired of what you used to collect? Get rid of it. Is it in boxes taking up closet space? Put it out where you can see it OR... You get my drift. Getting rid of it means by any means—sell, gift, donate, pitch. (NOTE: I'm not a fan of the last one; our landfills are overfilled. Donate before dumping! And if

you're going to regift it, please make sure it's
something they want or expect them to do
the same.)

A collecting story of my own:

Children are natural collectors. Take any three-
year-old to the beach and you will come home with
a bucketful of shells; some of them may even be
inhabited. So when my daughter was around that age
I asked her if she wanted to start a collection of her
own. She'd seen how much fun I had with my pottery,
so it seemed only natural that she had something for
herself. I've forgotten the details of the conversation
but we somehow settled on rubber ducks. We put
the word out to family and friends that if they should
stumble upon a rubber duck in their travels to please
send it our way. Who knew there were so many vari-
eties or unusual places to find them? They started
coming in from all over the world, from sporting
events (England's Olympic Cycling Team duck) and
museums (Spy Museum Sherlock Holmes duck) as
well as holiday locales (Germany's Oktoberfest duck),
in sizes ranging from grape to full-grown Pekingese.
She/we were blown away. At its peak, her collection
included nearly 70 rubber ducks all on display in her
bathroom. Over the years she has passed some down
to her younger cousins or gifted them to friends. She
even left a bunch behind for the new owners of our

house, who have a toddler and a preschooler. She has about half her original collection left and for the moment they are in storage awaiting placement in her bathroom once it's renovated. They have brought so much joy not only to her but to the people who found them on their travels and said to themselves, "She's going to love this."

I tell this story to make the point that I'm not anti-collections by any means. What I am is anti-obligation to continuing the tradition of gifting something to someone who doesn't really want it, ultimately resulting in clutter, wasted money and space, and holding onto things you aren't enjoying (either because you are not seeing something you love or you are being gifted something you don't want). Collecting should be fun! It is "joy in object form."

* * *

I met Tara's son in the driveway of her house as I was leaving that last day. He told me how much he and his wife loved the work that had been done so far and couldn't wait to see the finished product inside. He also suggested that they would love to have me do some work for them in their home. Then he asked, "Just out of curiosity, would you know how much those figurines are worth? They're not really our deal and one day down the road of course, I don't even want to say it but you know what I'm thinking, we'll probably want to sell them." Is it any wonder why I advise clients the way I do? This is why I say collections are meant to be enjoyed and not saved for someone else at some other time.

9

I'm Going to Need You
to Help Me Help You

Client: (laughing through tears) *"I'm so in over my head. There are things from my mother's place when I cleared it out, stuff that the kids have outgrown, products from at least three different multi-level marketing companies I bought into, and God knows, I can't say no to my kids when they want something. They've been through so much. I'm a mess. I may be beyond help."*

BBT: (smiling sympathetically) *"Well, as the saying goes, the first step is admitting there is a problem."* (handing her a tissue with a wink) *Tell me, why is now the time for this change? What is your end goal? Then we can talk about the best way for us to work through this together."*

In the early days of my business, I would be overly accommodating. No matter the filth and regardless of the amount of clutter, I always said I could make it look beautiful. I suppose equal parts ego and inexperience were at play, leading me to think I could conquer any situation. That was my first mistake. Consistently underestimating the time and effort these jobs would take and subsequently, grossly undervaluing the cost of my work would be mistake number two.

Back then, there were countless days I crawled home exhausted, stripped my dirty clothes off at the door, and fell into a hot shower in an attempt to wash away the mental image of what I had just endured during the previous nine hours. I didn't know then that I really wasn't helping my clients or myself because I hadn't fully thought through what it was these clients were actually asking of me. They had called me in to organize their homes but what they were unknowingly asking of me was to organize their lives. All the superficial as well as the deep emotions that played into their clutter, their need to hold on, their shopping and hoarding tendencies, their need for approval, their hopes for a different version of themselves; it was all part of it. But I naively put all their issues into one box—disorganized. Mistake number three.

I remember one particularly grueling day when I finally woke up to the underlying problem of my business model: I was not requiring my clients to be part of the process. That was a glaring omission on my part. I hadn't taken the time to talk to them about what happened to get them to this place, or how they lived their lives in their homes, or why they weren't able to fix and maintain it for themselves. I was only thinking, "I can whip this place into shape and make it look gorgeous." But in only considering a beautiful Instagram-worthy reveal room, I wasn't fixing the problem at its core. These were people at various levels of disorganization, some modestly messy, some truly gag worthy. It wasn't in their nature to maintain any of the work I had done, and more importantly, I hadn't gotten to the emotional root cause of their issues with their belongings. Falling back into bad habits was an inevitability. Continuing to work with my original end goal would never fundamentally help my clients. I think I'm up to mistake number four.

In my defense, it is just this sort of focus on before and after photos and making for a good social media post that makes most organizers ineffective. Not to badmouth my colleagues in this field, but even I couldn't live inside a home that looks like those glossy pictures, and everything in my house is at near perfect right angles. No one can expect someone who once lived in chaos to magically live in straight lines with the help of calligraphy-written labels throughout their refrigerator. It's the very reason people fall off the proverbial wagon after all the work invested in paring down and cleaning up. As the quote from the Chinese philosopher Lao Tzu, founder of Taoism, says, "Give a man a fish and you feed him for a day. Teach him how to fish and you feed him for a lifetime." I no longer had an interest in feeding my clients beautifully refined spaces they couldn't live in. Going forward I only wanted to work with them to make a meal together that they could continue to make for years to come.

That day I created a new protocol for myself that changed the entire structure of my business and turned out to be the nexus for this book. A simple three-part plan emerged:

1. **I would require the investment of sufficient initial time with my client to learn how, what, and why they were living this way.**

2. **I would require mutual involvement on the part of my client to downsize their clutter, to learn the method in my process, and to cultivate better lifestyle habits so they would be better able to keep it that way once I'd left.**

3. **And without complete compliance from the client regarding both of the above, I would not be taking on the project.**

It was a drastic shift in focus, but it had become monumentally important for both me and for my clients that the appropriate expectations should be set at the start. If a client was unwilling to participate, I was unwilling to invest the time. But those who accepted my requirements gained far more than a short-lived organized home. They learned about themselves, their role in creating the mess, and their ability to reshape the way they lived so their lives weren't spent looking for or walking around their belongings. I had to remain steadfast in my new commitment to improve the lives of my clients through instruction and a bit of introspection.

Going forward, I would have to say no to some potential clients. Ones who were unwilling to let go of any of their belongings even when it was obvious their possessions were taking up the bulk of their living spaces. Or ones who were just looking for a day laborer to implement their misguided plans. Or ones who were beyond my help and needed a therapist experienced with hoarding, a hazmat crew, and a fleet of dumpsters.

I would also have to make very clear that this was a shared process between me and them. How they used the space and how their family lived were questions I would need answers to in order to create a plan of action. The plan would not only be for how to streamline the space but how to use it in order to maintain its efficiency. I would not only be organizing the space but teaching them how to live organized lives in the process. This wasn't an exercise in getting it all to look like the bedding department at Bloomingdales, crisp folds of cotton in a rainbow of muted ombre shades.

This was about making efficient spaces for less-than-efficient people and giving them the tools to keep it that way.

* * *

Onto my story. Claire was a friend of a friend. All our kids took karate lessons together so we often saw each other in the evenings while waiting for class to finish. We started chatting one day and she asked if I would consider coming to her house to see if there was anything I could suggest "for a single working mom of two crazy kids, who couldn't pay you." I laughed and said I'd be happy to come by and give her some advice. She apologized in advance for the disaster that awaited my visit saying she was "beyond embarrassed" and that she had "completely lost control." When I saw her home later that week her stories of the colossal chaos were not exaggerated.

Imagine a typical three-bedroom, two-and-half bath, mid-'70s suburban house. Worn paint, dated decorative details, weeds pushing through the asphalt of the driveway. Now imagine being met at the door by moving boxes, layers of multiple seasonal and holiday decorations, kid and pet toys, errant dirty dishes and cups, and discarded coats and shoes, all topped with dust and dog hair. And that was just the foyer. This visual cacophony extended through the entire house. This was a monumental undertaking and not something she was going to be able to accomplish without a team and a few weeks of working nonstop. She was so clearly uncomfortable that there wasn't somewhere clean to sit down that she started to glow with sweat. I thought a distraction would be timely.

"Claire, you know what, I'm dying for a Starbucks. Come on, let's go and chat there. My treat." She was visibly relieved.

Once sitting, coffee in hand, I asked her to tell me her "story." Just a little about her life in the hopes of finding out what led her to this place. A house like that doesn't happen overnight and if I was going to give her the right tools to overcome her clutter on her own, I needed to know more about how it happened. The more she told me, the more I realized she needed this organization as a way to clear her life far more than as a need to clear her home.

I wish I could say her story was unique but I've heard and seen it all before. She was married with two young boys when her husband left her for someone else. He claimed he was destitute so the court ruled he did not have to give her alimony and the child support he was required to pay covered next to nothing. She was a secretary in a dental office and had been training to be a hygienist, but she'd had to give up school because she couldn't justify the cost of classes and she hadn't had the time to study since she was the sole parent. She was barely covering the cost of her mortgage and she often went hungry so her boys could eat. As for the karate lessons, it was our mutual friend who paid the fee.

The house was given to her in the divorce but it was falling into disrepair and she couldn't afford to have it fixed. She knew selling it was the smart choice but she couldn't see past the clutter and issues to wrap her head around preparing it for sale, much less move two boys from the only home they'd known. Then there were the two dogs. She thought about giving them up for adoption but the boys had been through so much in the last few years she couldn't bring herself to take them away even though between food and vet bills, they had become a burden. Her guilt over the divorce and not spending enough time with her boys was another reason she never said no to a toy or video game if they asked, even though she knew she might max out her credit cards, which on most days were the only way she could put food on the table. And in the process of all this, her mother had passed away, leaving her to clear out the condo her mother rented and bring all the belongings into her home.

I just sat and listened. She obviously needed to unburden herself of all this baggage she was carrying. My heart broke for her situation. I was happy to be of any help to her that I could, and when we both realized it was time to pick the kids up from school, I promised her I would spend the next few days trying to come up with a plan to make her living situation easier. But I also felt that in everything she had said that she wasn't fully committed to the work that lay ahead. She mused more than once that she just wanted to wake up to "a brand new life where everything is perfect," and life would be so much easier if she just found "a rich guy to marry and take care of me and the boys."

"Sorry babe. Life doesn't work like that. But just think how great it will feel when *you* handle this all on *your* own for *yourself*. So empowering! To think that even just a few months from now, your life could be on a path to a completely different reality of your own making. Then you'll not only be living this amazing life, but you get to take the credit for it! You'll wake up every day in your beautiful home and start your well-orchestrated morning routine. Right now, I am envisioning you and boys skipping out the door. It's in my head clear as day! You, coffee in hand, them with their backpacks and lunch boxes filled with Grade A homework and meals to match," I said with a laugh as I collected my things to go.

"Yeah, it does sound good. But the dream would be nice too," she replied.

The process of downsizing and organizing, frankly the process of anything you do that changes your life, takes commitment and focus and work. Lots of work! But really, how many opportunities is one presented with where the work involved is in direct proportion to the result? An investment in yourself! And you get to take all the credit. That's a true reward for a job well done. And every day, every stinkin' day, you have the same opportunity to create the life you truly want for yourself. I know and believe that. But it's not something you can dream about and it happens (if that were the case I'd be at least four inches taller).

This was not something I was going to dedicate more energy to than she was, so I did what I promised and came up with a plan. A plan I would not help her implement until she was ready to put in the work of actually making it happen for herself.

LIST I SENT TO CLAIRE:

→ **Know your goals and what is driving you to achieve them.** Maybe your goal is to get your house in order so you can sell it. Or maybe it's so you can find your earrings in the morning. Either way, it must be big enough to keep you motivated to get the job done.

→ **Create a calendar of work to be done,** ideally with some time off from your job so you can work uninterrupted while the boys are in school.

→ **Have an honest and frank discussion with the kids** about spending, taking on some responsibilities, keeping the house clean, taking care of the dogs, and saving for big future purchases like vacations.

→ **Enlist friends, family, fellow church members, coworkers, and neighbors to help.** It takes a village.

→ **Tackle downsizing excess belongings room by room,** starting in the rooms that do not get much use. If you start with the rooms you live in most, you'll be constantly redoing them.

→ **Tackle finances** by selling off excess belongings, paying down credit card debt, saving for large ticket items like house repairs, stopping frivolous spending on things for the kids, and finding ways to increase income perhaps from additional income streams.

She called me to say she was concerned because it seemed like a tremendous amount of work and that again, she couldn't pay me. I said she didn't have to pay me because all I was giving her was advice and realistically, this was just the tip of the iceberg.

"Oh. OK. Well, I'll work on this and get back to you when I'm ready," she said, hesitantly.

"Sounds good. Let me know if you have any questions."

Oftentimes, staying in the current situation, no matter how lousy, seems preferable to the fear of moving forward into uncertainty. I hoped Claire would get back to me ready to jump in with both feet and a broom but I knew it would likely take more than a pep talk over coffee to move her from fantasizing about her mess magically getting fixed to taking charge of her life. The anxiety of having hard discussions with her children, changing the way she spent money, and being prepared for some labor-intensive work would likely prove no match for the "ease" of staying in the familiar. Even if the familiar was, to put it bluntly, gross. But change is difficult and human history is filled with people who have avoided difficult situations by staying in worse ones.

After nine chapters, it should be easy to see that I get excited about organizing. It's a rush for me, I'm not going to lie. Sometimes I get so wrapped up in the planning and implementation that goes into turning chaos into coordinated that I don't fully appreciate that my client is not as enthusiastic as I am. All I see in that moment is them living this efficient and beneficial life that I helped them create for themselves. Man, that sounds egotistical! That's yet another mistake I suppose and at this point I've lost count. It's just that I want so badly for the person asking for help to move beyond their bad situation. But they have to get to their turning point in their own time. And I have to learn some patience.

Claire got back to me a few weeks later and asked if I would grab a cup of coffee during the kids' next karate class. We planned to meet up at a nearby Dunkin' Donuts and when I got there she was already seated with two cups of coffee and a notebook.

"What is all this? You are positively glowing," I said, taking off my coat and sitting down across from her.

"I'm ready. Just not *ready*, ready," she said, pushing my cup towards me.

"OK. Talk to me. What are you thinking?"

As I drank my coffee and listened, she told me that when I got back to her with a plan so quickly she was shocked. She half expected me to say it was all too much to be fixed, thus giving her an excuse to not do anything at all. But since that wasn't the case, she was exhausted just thinking about the work and the time involved. She knew she had to do something but she just didn't want to.

"I wanted you to say it was too big a mess and it couldn't be done because then I could just tell myself that if a professional couldn't manage to tackle it then I certainly didn't have a prayer of doing it," she said with a laugh.

"Well, it can be done but it's still your house. You don't have to do anything if you don't want to," I said, taking a sip of coffee.

"No. No. I'm getting to that part. I want to. I need to. But I can't take any time off of work so I need to do this in stages. That's why I brought this," she said, opening the notebook and smoothing out a page. "What's my first step?"

"Your first step is actually pretty fun. You're just going to **envision the life you want for yourself and then make a list.** Here, write this down."

1. **Close your eyes and let your mind wander to a picture of the life you want for yourself. It's like a vision board in your mind. If you fall asleep (which I do regularly using this technique), when you wake up try to go back and recreate the vision in detail.**

2. **Focus on what appears in your imagination. Move from room to room. Pay attention to every detail. Focus on how it makes you feel. Observe how it all functions and how the people in your life work within the vision.**

3. **When the vision is crystal clear, open your eyes and write it all down in list form, prioritizing nothing. Just write each random detail as it comes to you. Write it down in bullet point fashion. Be as descriptive as possible with your words.**

4. **With your list complete, look it over and write next to each point how it made you feel, who if anyone was in the vision, whether you were there and what you were doing. Explain why that vision and the feelings it gave you is important to you.**

5. **Lastly, if you have some thoughts on the subject, go ahead and write down some**

broadstroke planning—any notes on how to move forward toward accomplishing your vision.

"I have one stipulation. You are not to make a list of what you think you should say. I don't want a list of goals you think I want to see. You are to write only what makes sense for you, your boys, and the life you are building from this moment forward. I will help you with the plan afterwards so I don't want you to bog yourself down with how to accomplish any of this. Truthfully, this is an exercise in getting in deep with who you are."

* * *

This **"what, why, how" list technique** is one I do regularly for almost every goal I set for myself. Remember back to Chuck's chapter. Your "why" is your motivation. Without it, you most likely will not achieve your "what." Let me give you an example from my own home:

WHAT: We're heading into spring and the courtyard of my new home needs a ton of work. I can envision it with an outdoor sofa, lots of comfy cushions and footstools, brightly glazed pots filled with staked vegetables, climbing morning glories on the fence, and a workbench for potting herbs. I see my daughter and myself reading under the shade of an umbrella and friends over for Sunday brunch alfresco with a huge vase of fresh-cut flowers from my own cutting garden on display.

WHY: It's welcoming and comfortable and lush and pristine and it makes me feel a warm glow and in touch with nature. I want that for myself and I want to share it with those closest to me, enjoying my new home and this next phase of my life.

HOW: Currently, it's overgrown and lacks a clear vision (in fact, it looks a little like Sleeping Beauty's castle once the kingdom fell asleep). I can do the work myself over time or I can hire people to do the bulk of the cleanup and then plant and decorate on my own. I can call in a few landscapers for quotes but also attempt some of the tasks myself to cut down on the overall cost. I can use furniture and pots I already have, live with it for a while, and then determine what else I might need before making purchases. And I will remind myself that the beautiful end goal vision is not the only joy. The work and effort to bring my vision to fruition is just as important and joyful. And empowering.

* * *

Claire stopped writing and looked up at me with an expression that could only be described as elated trepidation. "I'm excited and scared," she said, laughing.

"It's going to be great. You've got this. Get the kids involved too. No reason they shouldn't be part of the vision and the planning. You guys are a team of three! But don't be pressured. In your own time, let yourself seriously think about it and get excited about it. A year from now, you and the kids can be living a completely different, better life."

Without saying a word, a huge smile crossed her face.

"Now," I said, "if you finish that and still have the energy, **make yourself a list of all the things that need to be repaired around the house.** I wish I knew sooner that I could have saved thousands of dollars over my lifetime by fixing easy home issues myself. YouTube has tutorials on EVERYTHING! I'm embarrassed to admit how many times I paid a plumber to give an Allen wrench a few twists in the motor of the garbage disposal. **Fix what you can on your own. Then get some estimates for the bigger projects so you can start preparing a budget."**

Let me fast track this story because working with Claire behind the scenes took the better part of the next two-and-a-half years. In that time:

- She envisioned her goals both short-term and long-term.
- She wrote down her whats and whys and we worked together on the hows.
- She got the kids to do the same so they were all

working together toward both the family goals and their individual goals. Teachable moments all around.

- She fixed some of the house issues herself, then worked out a barter to pay the handyman from her church in both cash and casseroles.
- She had four separate, two-day indoor yard sales where friends volunteered to help her out. She repaid their kindness and generosity with pizza and beer and anything they wanted to take.
- She found an antique shop to buy the bulk of her mother's furniture and used the money to pay down her credit card debt.
- She had a donation truck come to pick up stuff on three different occasions.
- She finally decided to sell the house because it was too much upkeep.
- She continued to pare down her belongings whenever she had time to post on Facebook Marketplace. Whatever money she made went directly to paying down credit cards.
- Speaking of which, she stopped using her credit cards altogether.
- She got a part-time job doing data entry working from home a couple hours at night after the boys had gone to bed.
- The kids got so into selling off their stuff she joked that she worried they'd sell the winter

coats off their backs. Her solution was that they could sell almost anything they wanted to, but they first had to get her approval.

- I convinced her that the asking price of her house could be increased by having the house professionally deep cleaned. Afterwards, she and I worked to stage the house for sale. It sold in two weeks for the asking price even with a list of unfinished repairs.

- She and the kids moved into a townhouse closer to her work, cutting down on her commute and gas.

- I helped her decorate her new home with only those pieces she really loved and I set up lifestyle systems that they could all work with right from the start to keep it neat and running smoothly.

- The kids had tons of new friends in a close-knit neighborhood closer to school and found they played outside more instead of inside with video games.

- She was still working on the kids doing chores regularly but they were getting better, especially when it came to taking the dogs on walks.

- As a family, they saved money toward the family trip. Instead of Disney (which had originally been the dream), they decided on Great Wolf Lodge (close enough to drive to; all inclusive).

- And once things had settled down in an easy rhythm in her new home, Claire decided to re-enroll in dental hygienist classes.
- She still treated herself to her morning Dunkin' Donuts coffee twice a week, but had worked it into her budget. She hadn't bought anything new in a year and when she did buy something she needed for herself or the kids, she bought secondhand.
- She told me she really never felt deprived because she felt so accomplished in finding better solutions to things than spending money.
- She told me she and the kids were so much happier that it was worth all the work and habit forming and going without every little whim to get there.

It was a slow and steady process but she never stopped. I'm not sure when the light clicked on but once it did, she was fully committed to her new life. I respected that in her immensely. She was creating her own vision for how she wanted to live, and I was really proud of her. Each week at karate, she looked happier, lighter, peppier. The kids too. They were clearly getting into the spirit of things as well!

Before I moved out of state, I checked in with her. It had been a couple of years since we last spoke because my daughter had stopped taking karate. She was still working at the same dental office but was now a hygienist. The boys were doing great in school; one had even been accepted to the gifted program through the public school system. She was saving toward another vacation, this time to Hawaii, and she was excited about it even though it was a few years off. She asked me to stop by and see the house.

Neat and inviting. That was my first thought and that feeling stayed with me the whole visit. There was a system for coats and shoes, and a system for homework and chores. The kids kept their rooms orderly (for young teens) and Claire kept hers especially clutter free and serene. She glowed when she said, "You told me back then, a bedroom is for 'relaxing and recharging, not storage.' You were so right!" She did have a small catchall room on the lower level that she wouldn't let me see, but I understood. We all need one. And now that they had a routine down, they were considering a puppy since sadly their dogs were no longer with them.

"I am so proud of you!" I said, giving her a big hug.

"I'm proud of myself too! I remember that hellhole I was living in. I remember how I was always tired and the boys were so greedy. I felt like an absolute loser. And I thought I was going to be stuck like that forever. I never imagined this."

"But of course you did! That was the first step—envision the life you want. You did it!"

"Hey! I guess I did! Thinking of how I used to live makes me really anxious now. What a waste of time and money."

"Don't beat yourself up about it. It was all a learning experience. I like to believe that we all need to go through tough times to get to a better place. If life were easy then, you wouldn't be living your vision now!"

*   *   *

Claire's story is like many—multiple sources of clutter all amassed during the everyday living of a less-than-happy life, until there is much more than expected and no clear idea how to remedy it. I feel on some level that she and I were meant to cross paths at that time. Had I met her earlier in my career, I would have only been thinking of ways to make it look good. I would not have been considering how she and her boys lived and why they had clutter or mess, and not on creating a space for them or teaching them how to use it based on their lifestyle. I would have been creating my space and my habits, in their home. When I said to Claire not to beat herself up about it, I was saying that to myself too, for my many mistakes. It's all a learning experience. Growth and change are not easy but nothing worth it ever is.

Let me wrap up this chapter with an experiment. You've no doubt heard the phrase "my happy place." Now, I can guarantee with near 100% certainty that no one's idea of a happy place is a cluttered, dysfunctional home. Hotel rooms are clean and efficient for a reason. No one wants to be surrounded by a mess when they are trying to relax and rejuvenate (read that again). So why live like that the rest of the year? Why not live in your happy place? Let's go back to your image. Maybe you're sitting on a veranda overlooking the Mediterranean. Why is that your happy place? Is it the cool-colored hues of the sea and sky, the salty breeze off the water, the smell of lemons and figs, the laidback lifestyle of good food and expressive conversation, the crisp white sheets on the bed? Guess what? You can have all of that at home. You can create that lifestyle, those emotions, those scents and sights in your own home. But you have to let go of everything that's not in the picture. You have to commit to changing the way you are living in order to create the life you only think is out of your reach.

Imagine. You can live in your happy place not just on vacation but all the time. Envision it. Write it down. Make a plan. Follow the steps. And in less time than you think, you could live your ideal life all the time.

10

Stop Buying Bins!

Client: "I started organizing before you got here. I bought colored bins. A different color for each family member and I started separating the clutter. But these are already full so I need to buy more."

BBT: "You've got the start of an organizing idea in place so let's use it as a jumping off point. Before you buy more bins, though, let's work through what you have. Living with stacks of bins is not the end goal."

SIDE STEP: You've reached the last chapter of the book! Did any of the chapters speak to you personally? Overloaded clothes closet? Former Beanie Baby collector? You brake for yard sales? Maybe you just love your clutter and you couldn't wait to get to the end of the book to write an Amazon review that says "Bonnie, you can't tell me what to do with my stuff! I'm keeping it all!" To which I will reply, "Go for it!" But you read this book for one reason or another, right? I mean, you can't all be friends of mine who felt obligated to buy it. Admit it, you thought you might get something out of it. And that's exactly why I wrote it in the first place. Consider me your clutter whisperer attempting to explain what I've learned over the years so that you can help yourself. And regardless of how you came to this point, I hope you've found something that has changed your perception of your things and found a bit of motivation in the process. If not, I've got one last chance to convince you that clutter is cruel and putting it in bins to "organize" it doesn't fix the problem at all.

I have joked with clients in the past using over-the-top exaggerated hand gestures and facial expressions saying "STOP BUYING BINS!" What I loathe most about the concept of bins (and by that I mean tubs/boxes/baskets/bags, really anything that houses other things in a seemingly productive way) is that they're marketed as organizing tools. LIARS! The only way to effectively organize is to have less stuff to keep neat in the first place, thus negating the need to store said stuff in the second place, in an attempt to organize! Whew!

Now don't get me wrong, bins have their place in the world and I've noted several uses along the way. I personally love big, clear plastic storage bins as much as the next person, especially when you can see the neatly consolidated contents inside. Having them stacked in a dry storage area until such a time that their contents are used again makes me absolutely gleeful. But that's not why most people purchase them. No, most people have been fooled into thinking that if they throw everything in a plastic lidded box, they can call it a day on the whole organizing ritual. HELL, NO! All you have done is hide your crap. In fact, do you want to know what will happen once you put something in a bin? When you need that something again, you will either have forgotten it's in one of the dozens of color-coordinated tubs, or worse, you'll remember but just not want to be bothered looking for it, so you'll go and buy it again! What?! That's just more stuff! And why exactly has that happened? Because you put it in a bin out of sight, out of mind, to "organize it"! Please for the love of all things neat and tidy, PLEASE JUST DON'T.

I wish I were wrong, but sadly I'm not. The number-one reason for disorganization is more stuff than room. Why then would buying bins do anything but add to the clutter, even if it does appear to make it neater? There is no way around it. When it comes to organizing, if you have more things than space, some things have to go! Bins do not, won't, *nunca*, will never equal organization. Good God, I could rant all day about the stuff I find inside these well-intentioned bins, most of which is actual trash. I don't just mean "soccer cleats that no longer fit your kid" trash. I mean "empty McDonald's fries containers and grocery store receipts" trash. But I get it! Hands up in mock surrender. You've got a reason and a rationale for everything, don't you. And yes, nested bins stacked together in a tower are absolutely preferable to scattered garbage all over the place. But to be blunt, bins are the Band-Aid on the severed arm that is your clutter. They are not fixing the problem.

* * *

OK. It's storytime.

I had the privilege of working with a beautiful blended family. It was a second marriage for both Priya and Tom and both brought children to the mix, two aged 11 and 9, and three aged 18, 13, and 8, respectively. A year prior to me meeting them, they had bought a bigger house so the entire family of children coming and going between parents' homes could all live symbiotically under one roof on the days they were all together. For a home filled with so many opposing personalities, love between them all was not lacking. Neither was stuff. As is often the case with a bustling big family life and busy schedules, their house was only partially unpacked even after a year. Priya had called me in to help provide some guidance because she was tired of living with boxes and felt "in over her head." Literally in fact; the three-car garage (which had no room for cars) was filled to the two-story ceiling rafters with bins containing all sorts of household accumulations. Priya had attempted at least one marginally successful fix for the everyday clutter by lining up against the wall nearest the door to the garage a row of large, heavy duty tubs, each labeled with a corresponding kid's name. Since each child was involved in extracurricular activities, the bins housed sports equipment and musical instruments and well as coats, shoes and backpacks. It was a valiant attempt at keeping the clutter under control. Unfortunately, with a family this size, these bins were not a perfect solution. Can you even imagine a fourth grader searching for their bow rosin in the bottom of a 20-gallon bucket, one shoe on and the school bus driver beeping? I'm getting anxious just writing that.

When I first met with this couple, I had the feeling that Tom did not think an organizer was the answer. For the record, husbands rarely do, but by the end they are the first ones to proudly tell their friends they worked with a professional organizer. As suspected, he wasn't keen to have me tell him and his wife how to get their lives in order. Especially given that he was a military man. He thought Priya was being frivolous, and told her so sarcastically in front of me, and that she just needed to "get more bins to organize it." That was my cue. "How about we go through everything first and weed out what you don't need. The money you save by not buying more bins can pay my fee," I said with a grin. I was relieved to see him crack a smile.

Priya explained her priorities were with her makeshift mudroom setup, the garage chaos, and Tom's home office because, as she put it, "then he can be in there and stop annoying the shit out of me in the rest of the house." I love when completely head-over-heels-in-love couples rib each other mercilessly. They were enjoying themselves poking fun at one another and I was going to need them both in a good mood as we worked our way through this house. Win-win.

As a general rule, I start with the smallest space, but I felt Tom's hesitation to the process warranted immediate attention. He had his own collection of huge, black-plastic tubs housing everything from personal financial statements to memorabilia from his college football days to his awards from his active duty Air Force career. Lifting the lid off each container, it was apparent that he needed his organizing skills to straighten up and fly right. I know, that was terrible.

The office had built-in floor-to-vaulted ceiling bookcases, but aside from a few shelves lined with folders and office equipment, they were empty. There was a paper calendar tacked haphazardly to the wall next to an oversized desk that was set at an awkward angle in the room. The desk was covered with both piles and scattered paperwork. The room was sparse and impersonal yet completely lacking in efficiency. And the impressive glass French doors that led into the room were not enough to save its sad interior.

I began the process of opening the seven bins of medals, trophies, signed footballs, framed photos, and a whole lot of paper. As I have mentioned before, I do not handle paperwork for privacy reasons so after separating out all the items, I re-binned the paper-work down to two plastic tubs and pushed them to the corner of the room. On top of them I taped a list of sorting suggestions and the website for a local security paper shredder service; this is a one-sheet informational that I always have on hand to leave with clients. Then, I called in Tom. I asked him to look over the items lying out and to tell me which ones were of the most significance to display on this magnificent bookcase.

When faced with putting things on display, the objects in question take one of two paths. The client either finds it sad that they have had something that brings them so much happiness stored away all this time. Or they find that the importance of items they held onto is not as vital when faced with the idea of seeing them every day. **It's easy enough to ask yourself the same with regard to your own possessions. Ask yourself, are these items important enough to have on display? Do they fill you with happiness, pride, love, all the good feelings? Are they worthy of a place of honor, and a chance to regale guests with the story supporting them? Do these objects tell the story of you and who you are?**

Tom took the first path. It warmed my heart to see how much these items of significance and sentimentality meant to him as he smiled in spite of himself. I may have even heard a sniffle but I pretended not to notice.

"If you can make it look nice, I'd like you to use it all."

"I can and I will."

Over the next two hours, I lined the shelves and hung the artwork and rearranged the furniture. Then I called both Tom and Priya in for the reveal. He didn't say a word. He walked past me and sat at his newly positioned desk, swung his chair around to face the shelves, and admired his lifetime of accomplishments. Priya gestured to me silently to follow her out to the hall and once we were both beyond the doors, she closed them, turned to me and gave me a huge hug. "I think he's on board now. You were so right to start with his space first."

Priya and I spent the better part of the rest of that day walking through the house and discussing plans. By the numbers alone it was a huge project—seven people, six bedrooms, three-car garage, half-finished basement, and more bins than I cared to count (I stopped at 62). Even still, the pros far outweighed the cons in this house. For one, it was so huge everyone had their own space. Two, this was not a family of hoarders, they just had a lot of stuff. Three, everything was clean and well cared for. What they lacked were systems to keep it running with military precision, and as I mentioned they had a lot of stuff. Blended families always do. I've been in some second-marriage homes where both coffee makers sat out on the kitchen counter because each spouse liked their coffee their way. I try to make it work for all parties involved but there is a limit.

So where to start for Priya and Tom? First and foremost I needed to know how a family of seven navigated their day-to-day life. Priya was a stay-at-home mom and Tom worked from home, but every third month he traveled for work wherein he was gone for two weeks. During those same two weeks, his three children stayed with their mother. With fewer overall people in the house, we scheduled our big clearout for Tom's next trip, which was in a couple of weeks, but we didn't waste the momentum of the day. We needed to think through downsizing, lifestyle systems, organizing and finally some decorating, but for the purposes of this book we will focus on the first.

The first thing I was itching to tackle were those bins acting as coat closet catchalls. Since Tom had given me the green light to do anything Priya wanted, I started by **drawing up plans for built-in storage** along the back wall of the family room just off the garage. This was their main entrance in and out the house so without a mudroom, I designated this section for that purpose. Each family member would have their own section of a 15-foot-long wardrobe. Each section would have three hooks for hanging coats and bags, along the bottom fifth of which would be an elastic mesh gate so that musical instrument cases or sporting equipment could be placed upright without falling out. Below that would be a drawer for shoes (not all the shoes, just the regulars). Above that would be an overhead compartment for hats, gloves, etc. The back wall of each section just below the hooks would be a clear plastic hanging bag sewn into pockets of various sizes to hold those little things that always go missing, favorite hair clips, that previously mentioned bow rosin, car keys, etc., so they could remain visible, secure, and in one easy-to-find place. I suggested that there be no doors to hide anything so everything was easily accessible. Priya approved. I called my contractor, who gave me a price and scheduled a start date in two weeks. Tom happily gave me his AmEx. And we were onto the next step. The dreaded garage.

Attempting to employ my usual "start small" mantra came with challenges. I had to think long and hard about what the first move should be, one that was doable in a relatively short amount of time, one that was a buildable first step, one that would motivate us to keep moving forward. As monumental a project as the garage was going to be, it was possible to break it down, I just didn't initially see a way.

Priya and I decided to set up our working area in the rarely used living room. Pushing the furniture to the walls and rolling up the rug, we **set up two banquet-sized folding tables. This would be where bins would be used for sorting, downsizing, and reassigning.** We used the five empty bins left from the office overhaul for this purpose and we were all set to get a fresh start early in the morning. Just for fun before I left, we ventured into the garage to see if I could be inspired to a plan of action. Eyeballing the stacks, I told Priya I'd like to:

1. **Start with one car bay.**
2. **Clear it out.**
3. **Sort the stuff.**
4. **Find new homes for everything.**
5. **Run stuff to the dump and donation center.**
6. **Come back.**
7. **Sweep it out.**
8. **Be able to park a car inside by the end of the day**. Although I wouldn't suggest parking a car inside until the entire area was cleared. No one wants a box of crystal wine glasses falling into their convertible.

Done. **"Starting small" achieved.** I said I'd see her in the morning. She said she'd have the coffee and egg sandwiches ready so we'd be fueled up. This was going to be fun!

With a project of this scale, I was employing nearly **every tactic in my arsenal at once.**
- Getting rid of clothes that no longer served this family.
- Weeding through craft projects, school papers, toys, books, sporting equipment, etc., that the kids had all outgrown.

- Separating out the heirlooms and sentimental items to store correctly.
- Dividing houseware and linen duplicates after merging two households.
- Downsizing all holiday decorations to a reasonable amount.
- Gifting, selling, or donating wedding gifts that missed the mark. (Can we just agree that novelty wedding anything is tacky and a ridiculous waste of money? Especially for a second wedding.)
- Discussing a halt on all additional purchases until all belongings were inventoried.
- Creating systems to give the space order and usefulness.
- And then, organizing it!

Coffee in hand, we were ready for battle.

Priya and I took a slow and steady approach to the bins stored inside. Opening the three bay doors and thanking God it was a nice day, we **pulled bin after bin from the first garage space out into the driveway, determined what overall contents were in each, and placed them in different piles by common theme—housewares, photo albums, holiday decor, etc.** With our categories separated and employing the "start small" approach, **we brought into the staging area in the living room all the bins from the smallest pile first—toys**.

Once inside with four 20-gallon bins, **we opened each and laid the contents out on the tables. My instructions were simple:**

→ **Anything broken was to be thrown out.** We moved a big trash can from the garage into the house and lined it for this purpose.

→ **Anything with missing pieces was put to the side in an empty bin with its coordinated parts placed in a Ziploc bag in the hopes of finding what was missing as everything was gone through.** We did find several items with missing pieces but in the end nothing worth keeping, so these items were also thrown out.

→ **Anything too young for the youngest child or of no interest to any of the kids but still in usable condition was placed in a box that would be dropped at a donation center.** It was not necessary for our purposes during this project, but items that fall into this category could also be sold if they are in like-new condition.

→ **Anything of sentimental value, I suggested we put to the side in a separate bin for consideration after the process.** There were two favorite stuffed animals, one belonging to each of her children. I suggested that they go in one of two places—into each child's room or into each child's baby box. Priya left it to the kids, who both decided to keep them in their rooms.

When we finished, there were four newly empty bins, a trash can full of bits and pieces of old toys not worth salvaging, and a box with sand toys bound for Goodwill. I suggested she hang onto the sand toys and wash them up to use for gardening or even as picnic party decor/serving pieces. **Giving second life to objects that have already served their initial purpose is one of my favorite ways to continue their usefulness.** And how adorable, after serious scrubbing and plastic wrap lining, would a sand pail of potato salad look at a summer BBQ!

Priya was practically buzzing! So back to the garage for the next smallest collection of bins. That's when she noticed the empty section of floor where the toy bins previously sat.

"Oh my God! That is *fantastic!* Do you have any idea how excited I am to see the floor in here?"

"As a matter of fact, I do!" I said, grabbing a stack of two bins and heading back inside.

I could regale you with the ins and outs of the rest of the week, but at this point it doesn't make for very good storytelling so I'll just **break the rest down into list**

form. I do love a good list! Before we begin, remember the basics:

1. **Choose a section of the area you are working in.**
2. **Pull out all the contents of that section.**
3. **Sort into categories.**
4. **Bring the smallest category of items to your staging area first. Work up from there.**
5. **Sort this category, ideally downsizing by half.** Yes, I said half. We all have too much stuff. I bet you won't even notice HALF your stuff missing. **Remember downsizing means by any outlet to remove it from your home.**
6. **Put the items you are keeping back into the space to organize once the process of downsizing is complete.**

NOTE: In areas that are typically not temperature controlled (garage, basement, attic), if you see or smell mold or mildew, please trash the affected items immediately. Health issues can be associated with fungus and donation centers will not accept items of this sort.

Now are you ready to get into this. Let's move onto downsizing tips by category. Remind yourself of this often if it helps: *This is your home. You are not obligated to keep anything you don't want. No matter what!*

Sports Equipment/Musical Instruments

With multiple kids participating in several activities each, growing into and out of sizes and interests, there was quite a bit of expensive gear. Luckily, the second-hand market for such items is always a busy one, with parents trying to be encouraging of their children's interests while not going broke in the process of buying new. Likewise, donations to sports teams and music schools is always gratefully welcome.

- → **Anything overly worn or broken; anything that can not be repaired: TRASH.**
- → **Anything in usable condition that can be passed down to a sibling: CLEAN, STORE.**
- → **Anything in usable condition that is no longer being used and will not be passed down to another sibling for their use: DONATE OR SELL.**
- → **Any seasonal equipment like skis/poles and life jackets/boating supplies: CLEAN, STORE.** For this family, the intent was to create permanent overhead storage units in the garage at a later date.

NOTE: DONATE also means a gift to someone you know who is in need or could use the items given, perhaps a teammate, neighbor, or younger cousin.

Housewares/Small Appliances/Linens
For Priya and Tom, after merging two homes and two families under one roof, they had duplicates of nearly everything.

- ➜ **Anything broken or missing essential accessories; anything that cannot be repaired: TRASH.**
- ➜ **Anything in usable condition, but is a duplicate to something already being used in the home; anything new in the box but several years old: DONATE OR SELL.**
- ➜ **Anything in usable condition that could be used in the dorm room of Tom's eldest daughter, going off to college later in the year: CLEANED, STORED.**
- ➜ **Any formal china, crystal, silver, etc., in excellent condition, separated and re-binned for later discussion: KEEP OR SELL.**
- ➜ **Any themed linen sets that are no longer of interest: DONATE OR SELL, OR TEAR AND USE FOR HOUSEHOLD CLEANING AND REPAIRS.** But don't go overboard holding mounds of them.
- ➜ **Any seasonal items like patio accessories and heavy wool blankets: CLEAN AND REDISTRIBUTE throughout the house. If they are then deemed redundant: DONATE OR SELL.**

Children's and Seasonal Clothes

For the most part, Tom's children's things were with their mother, but over the last year of comings and goings a pile for each of the three kids had begun to accumulate. This, in addition to years of Priya's children's clothes, made for a substantial collection of bins. If I haven't mentioned it before, STOP BUYING BINS!

→ **Anything torn, stained, damaged, missing buttons: REPAIR, CLEAN AND PLACE in the appropriate closet, OR DONATE.** Most donation locations will take items of this sort. If the garments are in terrible condition they will likely be turned into scrap fabric, which is used in making rags, fiber fill for furniture, and insulation, among other things.

→ **Anything in usable condition, not being worn by any member of the family because of fit or taste: DONATE.** I know I sound like a broken record.

→ **Anything that was in usable condition that would be useful to pass down to a sibling: CLEAN, STORE.**

→ **Anything of significant sentimental value or familial importance should be PROFESSIONALLY CLEANED AND BOXED AND STORED within the temperature controlled home.** These topics have been previously discussed in the book. Please ask yourself the hard questions you may not want to answer when determining if something is valuable enough to hold onto.

→ **Seasonal clothes like winter coats and hats should be PROFESSIONALLY CLEANED (or machine WASHED at home if not dry clean only) after the season ends and STORED within the temperature controlled home. If, however, a growing child will likely grow out of an item before the following use, you may want to DONATE OR SELL.**

ADVICE: SELLING children's clothes online is best done with groupings or mini-collections of items. Either group items together by size, or group multiple sizes of the same item. For example, any assortment of girls clothes size 5, which creates a mini, preferably seasonal, wardrobe for one child, or multiples of the same white dress in sizes 5, 6x, and 7, which may be used for sisters attending an event together.

NOTE: SELLING, whether online or during a yard sale, is time consuming. You may not want to be bothered with it. I, in fact for an extra service fee, offer to sell any items that were cleared during downsizing because most clients do not want to deal with the process. You may want to consider CONSIGNING your items. Consignment shops (children's, women's, home decor and furniture) are everywhere and in many cases offer a 50/50 split once the item sells. All you have to do is bring the shop the items and take back what doesn't get purchased. Even then, you can leave it to be donated. So simple.

Holiday Decorations

Not just for Christmas anymore, holiday decorations can add up quickly because every month of the year has decor-worthy days. And Target and HomeGoods do nothing to curb a shopper's desire for more. Even I find it hard to resist the allure of bringing a new Easter Bunny into my house each spring.

→ **Anything broken or missing pieces; anything that cannot be repaired; anything not worth repairing: TRASH.**

→ **Anything not displayed in the last three years; anything you have grown tired of displaying: DONATE.** Or consider regifting. Holiday serving pieces with homemade or even store-bought baked goods make beautiful hostess or teacher gifts. Meeting a friend for coffee and shopping? Bring her an ornament or two from your collection. It's all about giving castoffs a second chance to be enjoyed.

→ **Anything that can be repurposed into an item for extended or everyday use: CLEAN, REPURPOSE.** You may have themed Christmas (Santa) and Easter (striped eggs) dining plates, which make them holiday specific. But if your plates are winter (snowmen) and spring (flowers) you could get a month or more of everyday use out of them. Give them more life.

→ **Any items of collectible value (for example, Spode Christmas china or Christopher Radko ornaments) that you no longer want: REGIFT OR SELL.**

→ **All items remaining should be carefully REPACKED by HOLIDAY, LABELED, AND STORED. *THIS IS WHAT BINS ARE FOR!***

Photo Albums and Assorted Photos

This is *never* a project to take on during downsizing. It should always be left for later when you can devote ALL your time to it. Priya, thankfully, had her photo situation well in hand.

"Clearly, photo albums don't need to be sorted to see what stays and what goes. It all stays. What we need to do, and just so you know this could be done the next rainy day we meet, is to go through them and label them with dates, and determine a place and way to display them. Plastic bins in the garage are not the way to go."

"Mine are all labeled. Tom doesn't have any of his own, so it's all really just mine. And believe me, I have labeled them within an inch of their lives."

"If that's the case, tomorrow we can start by pulling them all out, getting them in chronological order, and shelving them for display. Personally, I love a place to sit, pull out a random year, and just reminisce. What do you think about that space at the top of the stairs? You've already got a chair and lamp there for reading. I can have my guys come out and install some shelves in the morning. Wouldn't take more than a few hours. We can even use prepainted wood so no wet paint to deal with. I know I have some nice black ones from a previous project."

"Oh my God! Really? That would be perfect. Yes. Let's do it."

I am truly grateful for a client who appreciates my advice, accommodates the work schedule, and has the financial resources to get it all done. I realize those clients are 1 in 100. Maybe 500. So it did not go unnoticed that I was lucky to be partnered with Priya and Tom in finally making their beautiful house more family-life friendly.

Priya and I worked late into the evening. It happened to be one of the few days in the month where all the kids were at the other parent's house. Tom knew Priya (and I) preferred if he were out of the way, so he too made himself scarce for the evening by going to dinner with some buddies. By 7:30 pm, after my arrival at 8:30 am, we had gone through every bin in the first garage bay and were about halfway through the second. Exhausted and hungry, we ordered a pizza to be delivered and sat down to talk through what we accomplished.

"My entire body hurts, but good God it's worth every sore muscle," Priya said, reaching for her phone to text Tom what we had accomplished. "I can't believe it! A full year with that mess. Wait! What am I talking about? That's just a year in this house! I've had those bins forever!"

"And to think, before I got here, you were going to buy more," I said with a smile.

"Ha ha. Tom just texted back a wide-eyed-stare emoji. He is going to lose his mind when he sees it. Hey, what am I going to do with all those extra bins now?"

"Hold onto them for the moment. We have a lot of house to cover and we are going to need a few as we go through. In the end, they will be easy enough to sell off. You bought the good ones!" We walked out to the garage to close the doors and admire our hard work just as the well-deserved pizza arrived.

The rest of this story turned out much like the fairy tale romance that was Priya and Tom's relationship. We finished going through the garage in a couple more days, then took a break for a week to wait on the organization system installation. I bought her a huge whiteboard/corkboard to serve as her command center and had that installed as well. With that done, we moved onto the interior spaces, which meant downsizing each kid's bedroom. Plus, don't forget, as we sorted out the garage and the coat bins, more items had to be worked into the bedrooms. So with the help of my assistant, Jesse, we rearranged furniture placement for better flow and organized the closets and storage units, after which I met with each kid to explain how to use their new space. And in a teachable moment with each child, we "shopped from their stock" and put back only the decorative elements they really wanted to keep. "More for the donation center, Jesse! Better bring the truck."

Priya felt that after watching the work being done to the five bedrooms, she could handle the master bedroom, bath, and his/her walk-in closets on her own. I secretly wondered if she was too embarrassed for me to see her closets. Given all the days we worked together, I had never once seen her wear the same thing twice. She clearly had a lot of clothes in there. I was, however, proud that she felt she could take on the challenge herself and told her that I was just a phone call away if she needed me again.

The items she wanted to sell started to pile up, so between the two of us we sourced consignment shops to take them to since neither of us had time or energy for online sales. As for what was left, we discussed a rotating system of use wherein if something was consistently passed over, it too would have to go, but both she and I felt confident that now that the house was in place she could take it from here with the ease of a professional organizer herself.

SIDE STORY: In fact, Priya told me on that last day we worked together that if I ever needed an extra pair of hands, she would love to join me. She didn't want or need a full-time job, but every now and then, she thought she'd like to get out of the house and do something like this because, as she put it, "It's just so damn satisfying!"

A year later, Priya and Tom called me back on a few interior design and decorating projects—living room, dining room, guest house. I had a ton of fun renovating the bathroom off the back patio with grasscloth wallpaper in a Caribbean-themed color palette. But as for the downsizing and organizing part of our partnership, we were done and I could not have been happier for them. They were one of my greatest success stories, living in shipshape conditions with the buzz of family life humming like a well-oiled machine. And all three cars inside the garage.

* * *

WHEN BINS ARE USEFUL

- For storing HOLIDAY DECORATIONS; only the ones you will use again. Not the ugly porcelain Santa that your second cousin gave you as a gag gift.
- For storing CLEANED SEASONAL CLOTHES; only the ones you will wear again. Not the itchy sweater you keep forgetting to donate.

- For storing SPORTS AND CAMPING EQUIPMENT, TOYS, DRY PET FOOD, or any number of other useful everyday items that you use on a regular basis AND you consistently sort through as items become worn or obsolete.

WHEN BINS ARE NOT USEFUL

- When they are a CATCHALL for random items.
- When they are filled with items that ARE UNUSED, DIRTY, AND/OR BROKEN.
- When they are filled with things just to get them OUT OF SIGHT.
- When they are filled with PARTS OF THINGS AND/OR ACTUAL TRASH.
- When they are just TAKING UP ROOM and therefore adding to the clutter.

The basic problem is not in owning and using bins, it's in what you are keeping inside them and the constant purchasing of more as a means of organizing things you should get rid of. Bins gives you the impression that you are organized when all you've actually done is box your garbage. Open the lid, the problem is still there. You haven't moved forward away from your clutter—you've gift wrapped it. Your home should not look like a well-stocked store room of a big-box warehouse with ceiling-high bins. Free yourself of your stuff and you won't need to buy bins at all!

Extras

The Myth of Buying for the Person You Want to Be

I own a practice drum pad and sticks. My daughter owns a skateboard. Everyone I have ever known my entire adult life has owned a piece of oversized exercise equipment.

You know the saying "putting the cart before the horse"; the idea of prioritizing your purchases in the wrong order by buying something before you need it, or buying impulsively with the intent of using but most likely using only a few times and losing interest. Or buying and never using. Or buying and regularly thinking about using but still never using. Or buying because one day you're going to use it. Or... you catch my drift.

Even if the want is there, the drive, motivation, direction, and need are not. That purchase could have waited for a more opportune time. Now it's clutter. The allure of buying for the person you want to be is strong. It's like a myth that if you are prepared for battle with your sword and shield, you will win the fight—no matter that you don't know how to use a sword or shield and there isn't a fight in sight. That's not really how it works. It's a bit more involved than that. You wouldn't buy a wedding dress before even meeting your future spouse, would you? Well, maybe that's a bad example. I know ladies who have done that and I really don't want to go down that road.

Here's the thing. Yes, it's true that many if not all interests or hobbies require supplies of some sort. But all too often we purchase with the *intent* of using instead of the *need* to use and that small but significant difference is a huge cause of clutter.

Let me throw myself under the bus here as an example. I have always secretly wanted to play the drums. I thought that instead of finding an expensive instructor to give a middle-aged woman like me lessons, I would try to learn on my own from online videos first. But in order to do that, I would need a practice pad and sticks. Easy enough and fiscally minded to boot. Amazon two-day delivery and voila! Next step, find some videos and get to work. But I'm writing a book so that should take precedence. And I should really go to the gym if I'm not writing because sitting at a computer all day is not good for my circulation and posture. And really, if I have a free moment, I should be doing A, B, C because I so rarely get to those things. And now, months later, there is a film of dust on my drum pad case. Will I learn how to play the drums? I certainly want to, and I aspire to, and I hope to, but it doesn't look like it's going to happen anytime soon. But I'm prepared for battle if and when the time arrives... and I'm out $19.99 in the meantime.

What should I have done instead? One, wait until I could actually devote the appropriate time to the task. Two, research learning videos so I was ready to begin as soon as the practice pad arrived. Three, order the pad but only after asking around to friends if they had one they were no longer using (thus helping them downsize unknowingly). But I too fall victim to the myth.

Next time you want to learn how to brew beer at home or play the bagpipes and you reach for your phone to Google where to buy supplies and equipment, stop yourself and remember what comes first. It's never the wedding dress.

Things I Wish I Could Say in Reply When I Hear These Excuses

Client: "It's brand new! I just haven't used it yet."
BBT: "The receipt says 2018. Do you plan on using it soon or is it just for display?"
If it's never been used and you have no immediate need for it, you will more than likely never use it. It will

take up space, collect dust, and eventually age out of use. It is perfect, however, for gifting or selling. Pay it forward since you've already paid for it.

Client: "I can't get rid of it. It was a gift."
BBT: "I'm sure the person who gave it to you would be thrilled to know it's still in the gift box after all these years."
Here's a wake-up call. Not every gift you give is a hit. Not every gift you receive is, either. If I buy you something you can't or won't use, please return it for something you will. Barring that, regift it (I love a good regift) or sell it and use the money for something you want. My goal is not to burden you with clutter.

Client: "I may need it."
BBT: "If that ever actually happens, you can borrow it from someone because you clearly don't use it enough to own it."
I learned this one myself. I used to run to the store for every little need until I learned the joy of the borrowing system. I'm thinking about things like evening handbags for special occasions or gas-powered tools for that once-a-year yard cleanup. If you're not using them regularly, sell them. Both examples fetch good money in the secondhand market. If you need them again, borrow from a friend who hasn't learned the lesson yet.

Client: "It's still good."

BBT: "Great! It's much easier for the donation center to sell it."

When my daughter was younger she asked me why I was giving a particular puzzle to the thrift store. I said the dog chewed up a few pieces. And out of the mouth of this six-year-old came, "Then it's not good for anyone." Moral of the story: If it's still good that's good. Only give good stuff to the thrift store!

Client: "But I love it."
BBT: "Really? You've got a funny way of showing affection."

If you love something, set it free... from the box it came in, hiding in a shopping bag, in your hall closet. Show it off. Put it on. Use it up. Keep it well. Don't hide your love.

Client: "It's a family heirloom."
BBT: "Then by all means, in the corner of the garage is the best place for it."

What does that even mean? It's a family heirloom. Be very honest about what you are assigning sentimentality to. Your grandmother's housecoat with the rolled-up tissues in the pocket is not an heirloom... though admittedly, writing that does remind me of my Gram's housecoats. But no, having them hanging in one of my closets would not make that memory any sweeter. I will offer this up, though, now that I'm thinking about it. I wouldn't mind having her housecoats to

217

cut the fabric for bandanas to tie back my hair when I'm gardening. That's putting value to something that otherwise serves you in no way. Do you have family heirlooms? Pull them out and give them a second life! Or move them along.

Client: "I'm holding onto it for sentimental reasons."
BBT: "Not sure a cardboard box on the floor of your unfinished basement is the best place to keep those sentiments dry and damage free."
I get you! I myself have every letter from my first love tucked away in a steamer trunk inside my house. Notice "in what" and "where" I said those letters were. Respect the things you love.

Client: "I paid good money for that!" Likewise, *"I bought that on sale."*
BBT: "Money well spent, indeed."
I didn't write this quote but it is incredibly appropriate: "Look around. All that clutter used to be money. All that money used to be time." Enough said.

Client: "It's valuable!"
BBT: "Ha ha ha, who says?"
Monetary value for previously owned property comes down to "what the market will bear." That means it's worth only what someone is willing to pay for it. Once you own something, unless it is diamonds of impressive clarity or a Birkin bag, it's unlikely to increase in

value. Most everything decreases, and almost immediately. So yes, nearly everything you own will fetch you less than you paid for it (and even less once you ship it to the buyer). Be wary of the word "valuable."

Client: "That was my mother's."
BBT: "And I'm sure she'd tell you to get rid of it too."
I mentioned in a previous chapter that I do not want my future grandchildren holding onto something just because it was in my house when I died. "Honestly, sweetie, you don't have to keep my toothbrush holder if you don't want it. Not everything is *valuable*."

Client: "Why should I just give it away?"
BBT: "It's not paying you rent to take up space here, is it?"
OK. You want to get defensive about your mess. Let's go. Prove to me that it's worth keeping. Why should you give it away? Don't think of it like that. Instead, give yourself permission to free yourself from the mistake of holding onto it in the first place. Stop gripping your clutter like a badge of honor. Admit defeat and move on.

Client: "I'm not getting rid of that."
*BBT: "Then use it. Love it. Treat it with respect. Don't just **have** it. That's called hoarding!"*
No further comment.

How to Downsize in 10 Steps

1. Why have you chosen this moment to downsize? Hold onto that reason. That is your motivation.

2. Are you in the right headspace? Positivity and a focus on your end goal are the only ways to weather the emotional and physical toll that lies ahead.

3. Make a plan. Write your goal at the top. Plot out a daily to-do list. List ideas for what to do with what you are giving up. Follow your own instructions.

4. Gather what you need before you begin. Gather tools, cleaning supplies, boxes, etc., before you start so nothing stops your stride.

5. Break it down to baby steps. Start small. Finish that task. Feel accomplished. Go onto the next.

6. Sort. Sort. Then sort again. Fine-tune each time. Don't burden yourself with doing it all in the first go around.

7. Piles are your goal. Trash, donate, gift, sell, keep.

8. Keep only what you use and/or what feeds your soul. Anything else is just extra.

9. Remember Chapter 1, If It Doesn't Fit, Get Rid of It. That goes for inside your house too.

10. Appreciate the process and hold onto the feeling of finishing something. It will spur you on to not only start the next task at hand and the one after that, but along the way it will change your life in surprisingly positive ways so you don't come back to this point again. Or at least not to the same extent.

How to Get Rid of Things You're Getting Rid Of

- **Repurpose**—That chipped coffee mug you keep avoiding in your cabinet would look so pretty with a plant in it for your under-the-weather neighbor.

- **Clean up**—Old T-shirts make great cleaning rags.

- **Gift**—That second whatever that you bought "2 for 1" would make a perfect thank-you, hostess, or birthday gift.

- **Swap**—Books are my favorite swap items. You will literally never run out of literature.

- **Donate**—There are so many worthy donation locations. Do a bit of research. Determine their donation policies and what works best for you. Then give.

- **Sell online**—eBay, Amazon, Etsy, Replacements, and Facebook Marketplace, to name just a few.

- **Hand me down**—Keep it all in the family and extend it to your friends as well.

- **Parties**—Next girls night, have everyone bring their old accessories (jewelry, scarves, bags, unused makeup) and swap. Or use what surplus you have as party favors.

- **Events**—Is your child's school asking for donations of items for the next fundraiser? Check what you have on hand that's new or nearly and give that.

- **Auctions**—Do you have a houseful of furniture that needs new homes? Estate sales and/or auction houses may be an option for you. Check out local dealers for their list of services and their percentages.

- **Yard sales**—Throw it on the lawn with a sign reading $1 and you'll be asked if you have more inside.

- **Consign**—Consignment shops are popping up everywhere and they sell everything. Again, check what the percentages are and what sells best for them.

- **Gift to specific locations**—Gently used children's books are welcome at most elementary schools and children's hospitals. Ask what their safety and sanitation policies are.

- **Neighborhood listservs/clubs/groups**—Are you a member of any organization? Offer up your wares to them first. There may just be someone looking for something you are looking to unload.

- **Buy secondhand**—If you need to buy, try secondhand first. The same thrift store at which you dropped off your nearly-new never-worns will have someone else's that may be just what you're looking for. One man's trash is another man's treasure.

Everyday Tips to Minimize
Extra: Lifestyle Systems

SHOP FROM YOUR STOCK

- Out of toothpaste? Check your travel toiletry bag for the one you keep there and use it before it expires.
- Daughter or son needs a trifold board for a science project? Reuse the flip side of last year's. You can even cover the used part with wrapping paper.
- Notice a need for more light where you sit to read in the evening? Walk around the house to find an underused lamp somewhere else and move it to your nook.
- Think you need more plastic bins to corral your clutter? Think again.

There are a million ways to make what you already have work for you. Immediately buying new is not the answer. And here's the thing. There is literally no harm in trying to make what you have work. If it doesn't go as planned, there is still a big-box store somewhere where you can find what you're looking for. But try! Really try to solve your issue with what you have on hand first. It's actually kind of fun. I don't think that it will come as any surprise that my daughter got the biggest compliments from classmates in elementary school when she had random iron-on patches on her clothes, which she proudly explained were there covering up stains.

GIVE TO GET

- The next time your child wants a new toy, have them choose one (or more) that they no longer play with to donate first.
- Before you add to your library of books, sell a few online that are not worthy of keeping.
- Has the family grown through all the hand-me-down winter coats so that even the youngest kid is too big for them? Offer them to neighbors with little kids before you go shopping.

"You've Got to Give to Get" and "Two for One" have been mantras in our house for decades. My daughter rarely asks for anything without coming to me arms laden with castoffs. If she wants new clothes she's got a bag of clothes in hand ready for the donation center. If she wants new books, there is a box of books at the door bound for the little free library or to give to friends. Video games? She doesn't even bother to ask for those anymore. She sells hers on eBay when she no longer plays them and when she's earned enough in sales, just turns around and buys something else. This creates a recycling system of in and out items that never go beyond the current inventory at any one time. And at no point is there any feeling of deprivation, only charity.

SWAP, BARTER, BORROW

- Are you bored with your table linens and your friend says the same? Exchange them for the moment or forever.
- Could you use some help planting your vegetable garden? Offer your helper the first pick of the harvest.
- Going to a formal party and need an evening wrap? Ask your neighbor if she minds lending you hers.

I clearly sound like a broken record but it all bears repeating. DO NOT BUY what you can SWAP, BARTER, or BORROW. Even if it's something you think you'll use more than once, unless you are consistently in need of it, it's just not worth owning. This is not just an exercise in reducing and limiting your clutter. It's an exercise in community and friendship and charity and helping your fellow human. It's about slowing down the rate of production of new goods and using what we have in new ways. It's about putting less into landfills and keeping more money in our pockets. It's about prioritizing each other and the world we share rather than purchasing things. Every little bit helps.

I Used to Blog

In 2009, I started a blog about the random musings/ rantings of a stay-at-home mom. It's embarrassing to read now; I complained about nothing, A LOT. One of my posts, though, was the early workings of what would become my business. And the advice in it has stood the test of time.

Post from September, 2009
Show of hands, how many of you have a junk drawer? How about a junk closet? Shall we go a bit bigger and say a junk room? Do you have an entire level of your house filled with junk? Or are you, please say no, paying to store your junk someplace else? Now, how many of you would like NOT TO? Here are the tried-and-true basics to organizing anything:

- **Divide and Conquer** Don't look at a huge project and become disheartened; break the job down into manageable tasks. For example: a closet not a room, or even a shelf not a closet. No more than 5 square feet at a time. You'll be amazed how quickly it goes. And when you need a break, you have a clear stopping/starting point.

- **Purge Until It Hurts** Let's face it, there is so little we actually need to survive. All the rest is just "stuff." Get rid of it. Don't let yourself be convinced that your junk is worth something; I guarantee you the warped 45s you have in a dusty (once under water) box in your basement is indeed garbage. If it were worth something, you would have treated it better. And don't let yourself believe that you "need" any item that you haven't seen or thought about in five years. If you needed it, you'd be using it.

- **Reduce, Reuse, Recycle** <u>Reduce</u> we've discussed—free yourself of your clutter, unless it can be <u>reused</u>. Is there a little girl down the street who could use your daughter's old clothes? Do you have a friend trying to get in shape and a treadmill you're not using? Do you have some wild, decade-specific fashions that haven't seen the light of day since "Frankie Went to Hollywood"? Halloween is just around the corner. Let these items have a second life, even better if it's with someone else. <u>Recycling</u> is the easiest of all; before it becomes trash, consider if it can be recycled. Remember that box from college with the empty bottles of all your first beers that you proudly displayed as art. Now the entire contents plus the box can be recycled—proudly.

I Believe in a Junk Drawer

I have a junk drawer in my kitchen. I'm not sure it qualifies as a traditional junk drawer since I know what's in it. It's filled with one-offs that have no other home—a box of kitchen matches, random chip clips, half-burnt birthday candles, plastic takeout cutlery, a couple of Sharpie markers, and a few hair ties (sometimes I get hot when I'm cooking and need to pull my hair back). A real junk drawer is a collection of discarded surprises. Sometimes I wish mine were that. Those are always fun!

Organizing a junk drawer for a client is the ultimate work break for me. Gives me a chance to sit down and rummage through. Not from a nosy perspective but just the joy of knowing it's going to be 1000 times better when it's cleaned up, guaranteed. I love pulling it off its tracks and dumping the contents out, sorting the items into piles (which is always my favorite bit), then containing the items in some way and putting it all back. I'm no longer embarrassed by what I'm about to say—it's kind of a rush. Talk about instant gratification!

What I think I love most about a junk drawer specifically is that it gives the owner an excuse to have items all in one space that have no reason being together in the first place. But it can still be neat and organized! Let's be serious, I'm not giving you an out to have it stuck in place with filth and expired coupons (actual story). I'm saying the pressure is off to give it a single purpose. It's not the utensil drawer. It's not the spice drawer. It's the leftover orphan items drawer. And it's absolutely necessary.

ADVICE: Do not purchase drawer organizers. They are a completely unnecessary expense. Use what you have: Ziploc baggies, takeout containers, chipped coffee mugs bound for the trash. This is your junk drawer. Get creative with your junk containment.

Now tell me. Don't you feel like putting the book down and running to the nearest junk drawer? Go! Do it! In no more than 10 minutes you'll be done. No grand planning, no expensive systems, just instant gratification! Then onto the rest!

The organization of an entire home can start with a single drawer.

My Philosophy

For as long as I can remember, I've been organizing and decorating. While other girls were busy dressing their Barbie dolls, I was rearranging the furniture in her Malibu beach bungalow for better flow. In the back seat on many a car trip, I would renovate the houses I saw out the window by visualizing new colored siding and landscaping. And just recently, a college friend reminded me that my dorm-room closet boasted color-coordinated hangers for each type of clothing (shirts on one, pants on another) and truthfully, I wasn't even fully aware; I just always did it that way. I still do.

When I started organizing and decorating professionally, the idea was simple: to help those overwhelmed by their possessions find a balance and an order that they could live their best lives in. Organizing our homes is transformative. Our homes are where we can be our true selves, where we seek both relaxation and rejuvenation. It stands to reason that a home that is both efficient and lovely will be a source of profound positive energy.

I am a firm believer that lifestyle must take precedence over precision. Maintaining efficiency is far more important than perfectly folded T-shirts. It is therefore essential for me to sit down and get to know my clients so I can create a space that works within their habits and lifestyle. All too often, I see organizers and decorators creating immaculate spaces that while beautiful, offer little hope that their clients will be able to maintain the look. There is nothing more frustrating to me than seeing the work of organizers and decorators who didn't take the time to get to know how their clients live. Worse still is that in far too many cases, organizers make the lives of their clients even more difficult by not only requiring military-meticulous displays but by adding unnecessary tasks to the routines. One of the worst such non-necessities, in my opinion, is labeling. Unless you are teaching a preschooler their sight words, please do not label up your house. It looks ridiculous! Honestly, if your Cheerios are in a clear container, you can see what they are. Better yet, just leave the cereal in the box it came in and put it in the pantry. It's already labeled. Rant over. Let me get back on track.

Clutter, and more importantly how it comes about, is personal. My clients may bring me into their homes, but by the time the projects are complete, they've brought me into their lives. I learn their habits and their lifestyle and how much or little they can or want to put into maintenance. I learn how they have accumulated their stuff, what is keeping them hostage to it, and why they find themselves in this place where they need help now. It's my job then to translate that information into a better living situation, focusing on helping them purge what no longer serves them, to put in place systems that will make their lives easier, and to create a decorative, livable environment that speaks to their tastes and habits. There is something so rewarding in seeing my clients' faces light up when they realize just how long they lived in a situation that wasn't working and how natural and easy it all feels now. That's half of why I do what I do.

Equally important to me is my hope that I impart a bit of understanding about the objects we all live with. Time after time, I see the same mindset in my clients; they are living in "lack." Lack of self-esteem, joy, belonging; a mindset of not enough; a sense of poverty. It's this poor mindset that attempts to buy happiness or success or status. I'm not judging. I've been there. And on the days I "need" to stretch my legs by "just window shopping'" I'm still there. I try to remind myself that I have more than I need already and more will not make me any happier. But it's hard to fight. We are programmed to believe that luxuries and things that mean success are bought. Then our consumerist culture tells us that whatever we own is not as good as the next best item up the food chain. And still it's not enough to have "next," we also must have "more." The play, of course, is to tap into our desire to have what makes us feel worthy. We don't want to feel lacking in any way. And here you were thinking you just wanted to get out of the house; you didn't know you were trying to buy away the insignificance you feel inside.

Do any of you remember the door-to-door marketing in the '90s whose ploy was to convince single women, in apartments no less, "Don't wait until you're married to get your formal china. You don't need a man for that, girl. Buy it now and then you'll have it. And you can buy those 12 settings on an installment plan of $19.99 a month." Can you even imagine the meetings those company executives had discussing the target demographic perfect for their offbrand place settings? Well, single shaming 20- to 30-something-year-old women aside, I'm here to tell you that between the 12 settings I inherited from my great uncle and the 13 settings I received as wedding gifts, my ex-husband and I each have complete sets that I doubt see the light of day more than once a year and then it's only four of the settings at most, not 12, not 13. So no one needs formal china. Want? Sure. I get that. But then for God's sake, use it and love it. Which reminds me. I think we'll have leftover pizza on Great Uncle Charlie's china tonight.

Anyone is capable of a beautiful home. There is no secret formula available only to the megarich or in monthly installments for the rest of time. You don't have to have a degree in design or be a DIY aficionado. You just have to have a home that works efficiently for how you live and surround yourself with things you love so that you don't want for more than you need.

Remember though, no organizer or decorator can fix your clutter issues if you are resistant to change. Ridding yourself of the stuff that plagues you starts with you.

STORY: I worked with a client several years back who had given me the keys to her home so I could work while she was away on business. When she got back from her trip I received this text:

"I don't know what I expected. But I didn't expect this."

I was so nervous thinking she was unhappy with the work but a few moments later, a second text came through:

> *"It looks amazing. I wanted to make a cup of tea and when I couldn't find the cups where they used to be, I thought, 'Where should the cups be?' and what do you know, that's exactly where they were. This is better than I ever dreamed it could be. Thank you."*

I love that story. We have since become friends and she has introduced me to other working women who don't have the energy to organize the homes they spend so little time in. Each of them has thanked me for making their lives easier and as a result they have never needed me again for more than a touchup. For better or for worse, if I've done my job correctly, I downsize myself out of a job.

Downsizing makes life easier. Organizing our homes makes life easier. Putting systems in place to keep everything running smoothly makes life easier.

It's really that simple.

I Know What You're Going Through

If nothing I've said has convinced you to stop adding to your clutter, let me leave you with this:

Say you have a goal in mind, maybe saving for a vacation home. You begin to save but something urgent comes up, car repairs for example, and you have to basically wipe out your savings. Now you're back to square one and you have nothing to show for your efforts (except a working vehicle, but that's no fun). Now you are feeling a bit frustrated and pent up, like you "need" some quick spending satisfaction, some prize for being so responsible to this point. Just a little treat.

A quick trip to Starbucks where you tell yourself you don't have a daily habit anymore so every once in a while couldn't hurt, and if you get the tall instead of the venti you just saved two bucks. Smile on your face and cappuccino in hand, you walk past a shoe store having a clearance sale. You check it out just for fun and realize that at these prices, you could buy 10 pairs of shoes for what you used to pay for one. But you don't need 10 so even if you only buy two (that you also don't need) you're ahead of the game. Shopping bags in hand and coffee gone, it's time for lunch. You have plenty of food at home since you just bought groceries (never detouring from your shopping list), but Panera is right there and you're in the mood for some hot soup.

Three hours and $60 later, you're home, stuffed, with

no room in your closet to put away those new shoes. More importantly, you're that much further away from that vacation home. And yes, this is my story, and no, I am not writing this from my grey-shingled cottage on Nantucket. And yes, I blame that on a lifetime of $60 treats.

I have since adopted the mantra "Saving Money One Unpurchased Item at a Time." I have less stuff and more savings. And yet, still too much stuff and still too little savings. But the path is clear. What is your path? What could you be saving toward if you weren't treating yourself to little things that add up? Once you begin to weigh every purchase against that end goal you'll find that saving is addictive and the space in your home is freeing.

I know firsthand. I have learned that lesson well. Every small purchase used to put me further away from my goal and many times added more clutter to the mix. That's a double whammy. I'm not sure when it happened, but when that switch got flipped it changed everything. As a result, I drink a lot of lousy coffee at home these days. A good 80% of the clothes in my closet have come from the thrift store. And my favorite wellies are wrapped in duct tape because they have holes in them that will soon render them completely useless in the rain.

But it will all be worth it.

I really want a grey-shingled cottage on Nantucket.

A Note To Booksellers:

Stop Buying Bins is the first in a series about efficient living and is specifically focused on downsizing—the natural first step in the process of organizing. I've been honing my decorating and organizing skills for decades starting with my own homes, then bartering with friends, before turning these techniques into a home organizing and interior decorating business.

I would be so grateful if you would carry this book in your store. And with prior planning, I would be happy to be a part of an in-person event.

I hope you enjoy reading it as much as I enjoyed writing it.

Thank you for your consideration.